FOCUS ON NATURE IN THE BIBLE

SNAPSHOTS

FOCUS ON NATURE IN THE BIBLE

SNAPSHOTS

LAURIE CHANCE SMITH

REVIEW AND HERALD® PUBLISHING ASSOCIATION
Since 1861 | www.reviewandherald.com

Published by Review and Herald® Publishing Association, Hagerstown, MD 21741-1119

Review and Herald® titles may be purchased in bulk for educational, business, fund-raising, or sales promotional use. For information, e-mail SpecialMarkets@reviewandherald.com.

The Review and Herald® Publishing Association publishes biblically based materials for spiritual, physical, and mental growth and Christian discipleship.

This book was
Edited by Penny Estes Wheeler
Copyedited by Vesna Mirkovich
Cover designed by Ron Pride / Review and Herald® Design Center
Cover art © Thinkstock.com
Interior designed by Emily Ford / Review and Herald® Design Center
Typeset: Minion Pro 13/15

PRINTED IN U.S.A.

17 16 15 14 13 5 4 3 2 1

Library of Congress Cataloging-in-Publication Data
Smith, Laurie Chance, 1969- .
Snapshots : nature stories in the Bible / Laurie Chance Smith.
p. cm.
1. Nature in the Bible—Juvenile literature. 2. Nature—Religious aspects—Christianity—Prayers and devotions—Juvenile literature. 3. Bible stories. I. Title.
BS660.S625 2013
220.8'508—dc23
2012032259

ISBN 978-0-8280-2689-5

Dedication

When I was a young girl, my mother gave me a small book entitled *Proverbs to Remember*. My favorite proverb was "Finding beauty isn't hard . . . It's always there in our own backyard." This book is dedicated to all the people who have helped me find God's beauty in my life:

Mom and Dad, gardeners extraordinaire
James, for walking the path with me
Luke and Joshua, who love the Bible and nature
Leanne, Mike, Brittany, and Cristal, for backyard adventures
the Smith clan, for welcoming me into the fold
Becky and Diane, partners, helpmates, and confidants
and to you, in the hope that you'll find beauty in your own backyard

Contents

Introduction

When was the last time you stopped to smell a flower blossom or paused to admire the radiance of the sun? Think of someone living in Bible times who, in another land and time, marveled at God's creation too.

The Bible is filled with stories about the natural world because spending time in nature brings us closer to God. Centuries have passed since the Bible was written, but the world of nature bridges ancient times to the present age. The Bible's nature stories provide living links to the biblical world. Trees and flowers grow today just as they grew in Bible times. The sun, moon, and stars shine in today's sky as they did in Bible times.

In nature we sense the same innate freedom that we find in having a relationship with the Divine. God is always with us on our faith journeys because our spiritual needs change moment to moment. Likewise, all things in the natural world change day to day and season to season. As the seasons change, plants put out fresh leaves and flower buds develop into blossoms. Year after year caterpillars gorge on leaves and spin cocoons toward one goal—to transform into butterflies. Every dawn brings a brand-new sunrise, different from the day before. Winds blow in new directions each day, and clouds float across the sky in an ever-changing pattern.

While nature embodies freedom, it also gives us evidence of the spiritual truths of joy, abundance, and order. When we hear a donkey bray, we can't help smiling at its loud, insistent greeting. The bright sun shares its radiance with everyone, and when we see leaves drop from the trees in the fall, we know new leaves will sprout again in spring. In nature all things have their purpose and direction. All things have their time and place.

The area of the natural world we'll explore in this study is called the Fertile Crescent. It is a crescent-shaped area of land that meanders along the shores of the Mediterranean Sea where important Bible events took place. Thus we will follow the Fertile Crescent, referring to the different segments as biblical geographical locations. The crescent begins in Egypt, where the Israelites were enslaved for more than 400 years. Ending this long period of slavery, Moses led the Israelites out of Egypt in what the Bible calls the Exodus. The crescent extends north to what the Bible calls the Promised Land. It then swerves over the Syrian Desert to Mesopotamia, ending in Babylonia.

The Promised Land stretched about 200 miles north to south along the Mediterranean Sea. From there it extended eastward about 50 miles to include the Jordan River and surrounding areas. Nature's scenery takes many different forms in the Promised Land: grassy plains, dry deserts, lakes and rivers, and valleys with plenty of water for growing crops. Mountains rise to 3,000 feet above sea level. The Dead Sea is the lowest point on the landscape, at 1,300 feet *below* sea level. Other names Bible writers have used to refer to the Promised Land include Zion, Holy Land, Canaan, Land of Israel, and Palestine. The climate of the Holy Land varies from place to place and year to year. Some Bible stories occur in a lush Mediterranean climate in which dry, moderate summers turn to rainy winters. But desert areas receive little rainfall in summer or winter, and plant life is scarce.

As we travel the lands of the Bible we'll capture snapshots of nature, from the tiny mustard seed to the luminous stars in the night sky. We'll focus on the beauty and mystery in God's creation and use this sampling of the Bible's nature lessons as a springboard for further study. Each chapter ends with a Prayer Focus to help us invite God into our day, a Zoom Lens to help us further our Bible study, and an Action Shot to suggest one way for us to make a difference in ourselves or in the world.

Section One

Through the Garden Gate: Biblical Seeds, Trees, Flowers, Herbs, and Plants

I am the gate; whoever enters through me will be saved.
They will come in and go out, and find pasture.
—John 10:9

Chapter 1

Seeds: Sowing Faith

The seed falling on good soil refers to someone who hears the word and understands it.
—Matthew 13:23

Jesus is called by many names, including the Good Shepherd, Cornerstone, Prince of Peace, Messiah, Bread of Life, Rock, and Bright Morning Star. But Jesus' followers, or disciples, often called Him Teacher, for He spent a lot of time teaching people to love God and to love one another. Jesus often told parables, stories that involve elements from daily life to teach a lesson. And the things Jesus talked about in His parables were familiar to the men and women and girls and boys who heard His stories. He often told stories about things in the outdoors—sheep, shepherds, fishing, pearls, vineyards, and farming. Understanding the meaning of the parables helps us learn the lesson that the parable, and Jesus, are trying to teach. Knowing the lesson enables us to live happily, and that makes God happy too.

Read Matthew 13:31, 32. Which small seed does Jesus say is the smallest seed to grow into the largest of plants, and finally the tallest tree? It's fantastic when you think about it—that God has put within a tiny seed the possibility of becoming a beautiful flower, a tall, majestic tree, and even a tree that bears the kind of fruit *you* like best!

The same possibility Jesus saw in the smallest seed is the promise He sees in you. With Jesus in your life anything can happen! There is no end to what you may achieve.

When we plant seeds in the garden, we expect extraordinary things to happen. When we study God's Word, we plant good seeds in our minds.

Seed Scattering

When Jesus was 30 years old, He began His public ministry. It lasted only three years, but in those years He changed the world forever.

Jesus was a powerful speaker; He performed many miracles, He loved everyone

He met, and He spent a lot of time alone praying to God. Though He was born in the south, in Bethlehem of Judea, Jesus grew up in the north, in Nazareth of Galilee. Most of His ministry took place in Galilee. One day as Jesus was teaching on the shore of the Sea of Galilee so many people crowded around Him that He decided to board a small boat and drift out in the water.

Imagine that you are standing among the crowd at the shore. Wiggle through the crowd until you're standing right in front. Small waves lap at your feet. Listen to Jesus tell the parable of the sower (Matt. 13:1-23). Imagine a farmer walking outside on a sunny day. He has a big cloth bag of seeds tied over his shoulder and around his waist. He reaches into the bag, takes out a handful of seeds, and tosses them onto the ground. Some of the seeds fall on a gravelly pathway, and birds nesting in nearby trees swoop down and eat them almost as soon as they touch the ground. Jesus likens this scenario to a person who hears God's Word but doesn't listen.

Other seeds fall between rocks where there is just a little dirt. When the rains come, these seeds sprout quickly, but their roots have no earth in which to grow. The blazing sun scorches their tiny leaves, and the little plants dry up and blow away. Jesus says these plants represent individuals who believe God's Word but quickly forget it. When hard times come, they lose their faith.

Some of the sower's seeds fall among weeds. These seeds sprout, but weeds grow more quickly than baby plants do, and the little plants are choked out by the weeds. Jesus says these plants are like people who love worldly things, such as money or video games or movies, more than they love God. If you let your love for worldly things grow, it may stop you from growing in God's love.

The last of the sower's seeds fall on rich, fertile ground. These seeds grow deep roots and mature into a bountiful harvest. Jesus says they are like a person who listens to God's Word and allows God's love to be first in their life.

Perseverance and Patience: Lessons From the Garden

Have you ever planted vegetables or flowers in a garden of your own?

Gardening is a lot of work. To begin you must clear all the grass and weeds out of a plot of ground. Then you must spade or till the soil to make the earth soft and ready for planting. Sometimes you need to add fertilizer, too. When the ground is ready, it's time to carefully plant the seeds. After that you must regularly water the ground and pull any weeds that come up so they don't choke the new plants and keep them from growing. Pulling weeds is tiresome, but a good gardener keeps at it. They look ahead to when they'll have beautiful flowers or a good harvest of tomatoes, green beans, carrots, or whatever else they've planted. They keep that goal in mind and wait patiently for the harvest. Their hard work pays off when their trees bear cherries, apples, pears, or other fruits, and when they pick fresh vegetables, herbs, and flowers from their gardens.

Sowing God's Word

In the parable of the sower Jesus is sowing the seed of God's Word.
He tells us: *Open your hearts to God's love.* That's preparing the soil.
Listen to God's teaching and read His Word. That's planting the seeds.
Get rid of any thoughts or behaviors that don't honor God. That's pulling the weeds.
And last, *Show God's love to others.* That's the harvest, the fruit of your labor.

Prayer Focus

Dear God, thank You for Jesus' simple yet powerful messages. We choose to love You and to love others here and now. You claim us as Your children. Thank You for planting a seed in us and for accepting us as we are. We choose to allow Your love to take root in our lives. We commit to a lifelong journey of discovering Your truths and the direction You plan for us to grow. Amen.

Zoom Lens

Read Genesis 47:23, 24. The Egyptians were in the midst of a terrible famine, and there was almost no food left to eat when King Pharaoh put Joseph in charge of helping the starving people. These verses tell us that Joseph gave seed to them so they could grow grain. Find the math equation Joseph used to collect a tax for Pharaoh from the crop.

Action Shot

Take a trip down the spice aisle at your local grocery store and look for mustard seeds. Although we don't know if the mustard seed Jesus mentioned was the black mustard plant (*Brassica nigra*), the white mustard (*Sinapis alba*), or some other plant, all mustard seeds are very small. A teaspoon holds about 500 mustard seeds. Compare that to the size of the largest known seed, the double coconut, which weighs about 44 pounds and is about the size of a cannonball.

Consider how little faith it takes for Jesus' words in Matthew 17:20 to be true: "Truly I tell you, if you have faith as small as a mustard seed, you can say to this mountain, 'Move from here to there,' and it will move. Nothing will be impossible for you."

How will you put your faith in action today?

Chapter 2

Tree Tales: Faith and Stability

At least there is hope for a tree:
If it is cut down, it will sprout again, and its new shoots will not fail.
—Job 14:7

The third day of Creation must have been one amazing day!

"God said, 'let the land produce vegetation: seed-bearing plants and trees on the land that bear fruit with seed in it, according to their various kinds.' And it was so. The land produced vegetation: plants bearing seed according to their kinds and trees bearing fruit with seed in it according to their kinds. And God saw that it was good" (Gen. 1:11, 12).

Trees were the largest of the plants that God created. These giants were vital to life in Bible times and still are today. Trees provide nuts, fruits, and syrup for us to eat. They provide shade from the sun, and wood to build homes and schools and churches.

Read Luke 19:1-4. Zacchaeus had strayed from God, but Jesus called him home. What type of tree did Zacchaeus climb so he could see Jesus better? Let's look at other Bible stories about trees to help us climb closer to God.

Lessons From Trees: Faith and Stability

All trees begin as a tiny seed. Imagine a tall oak tree that drops an acorn onto the ground. Often a squirrel snatches up the acorn, carries it far away, and buries it. Rain falls on the earth, the sun shines, and eventually the acorn sprouts into another tiny oak tree. Its roots reach down into the earth to gather nutrients to help it grow. The tree's leaves take in the carbon dioxide that humans and animals exhale, and through a process called photosynthesis, return oxygen to the environment for us to breathe. Trees are crucial for keeping earth's environment healthy.

Mighty oak trees were valued in Bible times because they often lived more than 1,000 years. A tree's longevity makes it a symbol of faith. Imagine how deep and wide the root system of a 1,000-year-old oak tree can reach and spread underneath the earth. A tree like that, rooted in the earth, stands strong and stable even when storms and strong winds blow. When we root ourselves in faith, we feel as sturdy as the tallest tree. The seed God planted in us keeps growing.

The Tree of Life

The date palm is often mentioned in the Bible. Dates were a staple food in Bible times, and many suggest that the date palm symbolizes the tree of life in the Garden of Eden (see Gen. 2:9; 3:22). In deserts a solitary palm sometimes marks the location of a spring of water. Let's look at two important Bible stories about palm trees.

The Palm of Deborah

Judges 4 tells a story about a remarkable woman named Deborah, one of the 12 judges spoken of in the book of Judges. These 12 judges led Israel for about 325 years, between the death of Joshua and the coming of the prophet Samuel. Judges 5:7—part of the Song of Deborah—describes Deborah as "a mother in Israel," a woman God chose to lead the people during a great trial.

Judge Deborah was also a prophet, a poet, and a soldier. Deborah held court under a palm tree in the hill country of Ephraim. Under the Palm of Deborah, she heard and resolved disputes among the Israelites. Because palms symbolize peace, it is fitting that Deborah resolved problems among the people while sitting under a palm tree. Deborah spread peace. How can you show peace to others today?

A Carpet of Palm Branches

John 12:12, 13 tells the story of a crowd of people who spread a carpet of palm branches on the road to welcome Jesus to Jerusalem: "The great crowd that had come for the festival heard that Jesus was on his way to Jerusalem. They took palm branches and went out to meet him, shouting, 'Hosanna!' 'Blessed is he who comes in the name of the Lord!' 'Blessed is the king of Israel!' "

As you know, after Jesus died He was buried in the tomb of a rich man, but He didn't stay there! Early Sunday morning an earthquake shook the ground. Angels from heaven rolled away the tombstone, and Jesus awoke back to life! Now He offers His resurrection as a gift to us, for when we believe in Him, He shares His spiritual victory with us. Today palm trees remain a symbol of spiritual victory.

Tree of Symbols

"I am like an olive tree flourishing in the house of God; I trust in God's unfailing love for ever and ever," sang David in Psalm 52:8. In Bible times the olive (*Olea europaea*) tree was considered beautiful even in old age when its limbs became scraggly and its trunk twisted. Hosea 14:6 says that when a person draws close to God, "his splendor will be like an olive tree."

Olive oil is a symbol of the Holy Spirit. Psalm 45:7 says that those who love the Lord will be anointed with an oil of joy. The psalm's oil of gladness is probably olive oil. Read about another use of anointing oil in Luke 10:34: "He went to him and bandaged his wounds, pouring on oil and wine. Then he put the man on his own donkey, brought him to an inn and took care of him." The oil the good Samaritan used to help heal the injured man was likely olive oil.

The olive branch has been a symbol of peace since Noah's dove returned with a freshly plucked olive leaf and thus showed Noah that the flood waters had receded from the earth (Gen. 8:11) and that leaves had begun to grow on the trees. Olive trees still grow in the Garden of Gethsemane and Mount of Olives in Jerusalem. Jeremiah 11:16 calls olive fruits "beautiful in form." Olive trees blossom in May, and the olives are harvested in October to be used whole or processed into oil. Today olive oil's healthful attributes make it a popular addition to many recipes, including bread, pizza, pasta, and dressing for salads and sandwiches.

Gift-bearing Trees

When Jesus was born, the Magi brought gifts of gold, frankincense, and myrrh. Two of those gifts—frankincense and myrrh—are tree "gums." Frankincense and myrrh are small trees that grow in the hot, humid regions around the Red Sea. To get tree gum, farmers make a long cut in the trunk of the tree and strip off part of its bark. Air hardens the milky white juice that runs from the frankincense tree and the yellow liquid that oozes from myrrh. After a few months, farmers scrape clear frankincense "pearls" and myrrh's brown resin into baskets.

Holy Anointing Oil

In ancient times frankincense and myrrh were used for perfume, incense, and embalming the dead. Frankincense smells clean and woody; myrrh's scent is smoky. Exodus 30:23 preserves an ancient recipe for a sacred anointing oil that includes myrrh as one of the essential ingredients.

Spicy Sticks

Cinnamon is also included in the recipe for holy anointing oil. During Bible times cinnamon was a beloved perfume and incense. Sometimes women scented their hair with cinnamon. The cinnamon we sprinkle on hot toast comes from the bark of the cinnamon tree. In winter, use cinnamon sticks to spice up tea or hot apple cider.

Chapter 3

Ancient Blossoms: Joy and Simplicity

The grass withers and the flowers fade,
but the word of our God stands forever.
—Isaiah 40:8, NLT

Glance around your backyard or a nearby field of wildflowers. If the blossoms you see are anemones, crocuses, hyacinths, irises, lilies, or tulips, you're likely admiring the same blossoms that Jesus did as He walked the roads and fields of the Holy Land. The names we give to flowers today may not be the same as those used in the Bible, but biblical scholars and botanists can often guess which flowers the Scriptures mention. Whether or not we know the exact flower named by Scripture, the lesson in each story remains as important today as in Bible times.

Read 1 Kings 6:18. Which flower do you think Solomon chose as the "open flowers" carved on the inside of the Temple? Many other scriptures blossom with stories about flowers.

Flowers Fade: God's Word Never Changes

Isaiah, whose name means "God's salvation," is often called Israel's greatest prophet. Isaiah uses his visionary voice to call Israel to a saving relationship with God. When Isaiah wrote, "The grass withers and the flowers fade, but the word of our God stands forever" (Isa. 40:8, NLT), he was likely thinking of poppy flowers, with blossoms made of four to six petals. Each blossom has a short life—only two or three days. During those days the poppy bloom opens every morning and fades, or closes, every evening.

Nowadays the bright blooms covering poppy fields herald the arrival of spring in Israel's fertile Jezreel Valley. Perhaps Isaiah sat in a field of poppies as he thought of how the things of the earth pass away while God and His love remain eternal.

Desert Blooms

Isaiah 35:1, 2 tell God's plan for the future glory of Zion: "The wilderness and the solitary place shall be glad for them; and the desert shall rejoice, and blossom as the rose. It shall blossom abundantly, and rejoice even with joy and singing" (KJV). Wild roses do grow in the mountains of Lebanon, but the rose of Isaiah 35:1 may have been a daffodil, a crocus, or some other flower. Regardless of the flower, the image of God's love blooming in the driest desert remains a lovely image. For many people the sweet familiar scent of a rose equals love, comfort, and healing. When you need comfort, hear God's promise in Isaiah 66:13: "As a mother comforts her child, so will I comfort you."

Cooking With Flowers

Imagine the "rose" of Isaiah 35:1 as a crocus, a flower that blooms in many different colors—purple, blue, pink, white, and orange-yellow. The crocus usually blooms before any other flower of spring. In fact, you may see the bright colors of crocus against the white of snow. This little flower seems to shout joyfully as it bursts from the ground. It's similar to the joy we feel when we walk with God.

In both ancient times and today, the stigmas of crocus (*Crocus sativus*) flowers are made into a spice for cooking called saffron. Stigmas are the long, straight, thin parts of the flower that rise up in the center of the blossom. Crocus stigmas are usually yellow, orange, or red. Stigmas are sticky because they are the part of the flower that receives pollen. It's likely that crocus grew in King Solomon's gardens (S. of Sol. 4:13, 14), and the king probably asked the bakers in his kitchen to cook a saffron cake.

Lilies of the Field

Listen to what Jesus said about flowers: "Consider the lilies, how they grow: they neither toil nor spin; but I tell you, not even Solomon in all his glory clothed himself like one of these. But if God so clothes the grass in the field, which is alive today and tomorrow is thrown into the furnace, how much more will He clothe you?" (Luke 12:27, 28, NASB).

Jesus reminds us that we should have no worries. If we continually seek God, He will provide for our needs.

Guessing Game

Scholars are not sure if, in the verse above, Jesus referred to an actual lily. The lily family of flowers is quite large. You may have seen pink, orange, or yellow lilies in a friend's garden. Lilies are so revered that a Chinese proverb advises: "When you have only two pennies left in the world, buy a loaf of bread with one, and a lily with the other."

The creamy white Easter lily often blooms around Easter. Like all lilies, they start as bulbs underground. A green stem shoots up, leaves fan out, and eventually the lily blossoms. The Easter lily's white bloom is taken as a symbol of Jesus' innocence, purity, and hope.

When Jesus walked from village to village in the Holy Land, He probably saw beautiful irises. Some people guess that the lily of the field was the yellow flag iris, which still grows today in Palestine. Iris plants start as rhizomes that grow beneath the earth. Irises bloom in a rainbow of colors, and some are "bearded" with frilly edges.

The "lilies of the field" could also have been wild tulips. Tulips in the Holy Land were bright red. Today people grow tulip bulbs of many different colors and cut the flowers for bouquets. Then again, daffodils may have been the lily Jesus spoke of. The daffodil's common name is "Lent lily" because it often blooms during the season of Lent, right before Easter. The lilies of the field may also have been anemones, cyclamens, hyacinths, or some other flower.

Prayer Focus

Dear God, thank You for flowers. The beautiful flowers You have given us bring joy and simplicity to life and a glimpse of what Your glory surely looks like. Thank You for Jesus' assurance that You value Your children and provide for our needs. Amen.

Zoom Lens

A West African proverb says, "Repetition is the mother of knowledge."

In nature, flowers repeat their cycles over and over. A seed grows into a plant. The plant blossoms and drops a seed that begins the process all over again. Likewise, some scriptures are repeated throughout the Bible perhaps because we often repeat life's lessons and find it comforting to hear God's words again and again. Which Old Testament scripture is repeated in 1 Peter 1:24, 25?

Action Shot

Gather a bouquet of flowers to surprise someone you love. In *Gift From the Sea* Anne Morrow Lindbergh writes, "Arranging a bowl of flowers in the morning can give a sense of quiet in a crowded day—like writing a poem, or saying a prayer."

Visit a local garden center to look at the lily bulbs, rose bushes, and anemone seeds. And if possible, see these flowers yourself.

Chapter 4

Herbs and Plants: Leafy Lessons

Land that drinks in the rain often falling on it and that produces a crop useful to those for whom it is farmed receives the blessing of God.
—Hebrews 6:7

God planted the first garden "in the east, in Eden" (Gen. 2:8, 9). Adam was the first gardener, and a long line of biblical horticulturists followed in his footsteps farming the land that God filled with "every green plant for food" (Gen. 1:30). Farmers grew their own crops and revered the earth as a gift from God. Hebrews 6 likens the wise gardener to the spiritually wise, saying that those who wish to live fruitful, productive lives must soak up God's wisdom as the land drinks in the rainwater.

Read Genesis 4:2. Which of Adam's sons was a gardener?

Imagine tending a farm in Bible times, where crops of herbs and plants were used for money, food, medicine, and in certain ceremonies.

Green Money

In Luke 11:42 Jesus says, "Woe to you Pharisees, because you give God a tenth of your mint, rue and all other kinds of garden herbs, but you neglect justice and the love of God. You should have practiced the latter without leaving the former undone."

The word *Pharisee* means "the separated ones." The Pharisees were an ancient Jewish sect who kept themselves apart from anyone who might be impure. Jesus loves everyone and never excludes anyone, especially those who might be considered outcasts from society. In this verse Jesus tells us that it is good to give money to help with God's work in the world, but He also reminds us that loving God and loving others is our most important contribution.

Visit a local herb garden and find a mint plant. Rub the bright-green leaves to release its familiar minty scent. Picture a person in Bible times cutting the mint, tying it into bundles, and using those plant leaves as money.

The mint Jesus mentions in Luke 11:42 is so easy to grow that modern gardeners consider it a big problem. If you plant mint in your garden, give it plenty of space. It spreads rapidly by sending out horizontal shoots or runners called *stolons*. But if you need to keep mint's growth to a small area, plant it in a pot and allow its colorful, aromatic runners to spill over the edges. Mint can be used in a variety of ways, including as a medicinal herb; people drink mint tea to ease upset stomach or headache.

A Candy Plant

You have likely tasted mint in the form of peppermint oil, peppermint candy, gum, or toothpaste. In the 1870s an Indiana candymaker used peppermint oil to flavor candy canes. Different legends explain the reason behind the shape of a candy cane. Right-side up, it looks like a shepherd's staff. Some people say it stands for the Good Shepherd. Upside down, it looks like the letter J and reminds us to think of Jesus when we eat a candy cane at Christmastime.

Precious Perfume

In John 12:3 Jesus' friend and follower Mary showed her reverence for Jesus by pouring a pint of "pure nard" on His feet and wiping it off with her hair. The pure nard is likely oil produced from the roots of the spikenard herb. Mary's pint of nard may have been imported from India in a sealed container. We know by Judas' appalled reaction that the precious perfume was incredibly expensive (see John 12:5). Mary waited to break the seal until the exact moment she chose to anoint Jesus. Today people who work with healing scents (aromatherapists) consider spikenard essential oil a calming scent.

Mary seems to be the only person who accepted that Jesus' death was going to happen soon. The disciple Matthew tells the same story, and Jesus explains, "When she poured this perfume on my body, she did it to prepare me for burial. Truly I tell you, wherever this gospel is preached throughout the world, what she has done will also be told, in memory of her" (Matt. 26:12, 13).

Coriander: Manna From Heaven

When God led Moses and the Israelites from Egypt, He promised to provide for their needs. Numbers 11:7-9 and Exodus 16:31, 32 both describe manna, the bread from heaven, as being similar to coriander seed. When you visit the grocery store, look at a bottle of coriander seed to get an idea of what manna may have looked like. The manna that fell from heaven could be eaten raw, but it could also be ground or crushed, cooked, and made into loaves. Scripture says it tasted like something made with olive oil or honey. Today coriander seed remains a popular cooking spice alongside cilantro, the leaves from the same plant.

Throughout the 40 chapters of Exodus we see that God kept His promises to the Israelites, even though they doubted Him many times. God has a plan for a fresh beginning for His people. He never gives up on them and never fails to provide for their needs.

Second Corinthians 9:8 reminds us, "God is able to bless you abundantly, so that in all things at all times, having all that you need, you will abound in every good work."

Cumin: A Spice for Time and Place

Cumin is an annual plant that grows wild in the Mediterranean region. The seeds, which are beaten off the stalks with a stick, are a common spice in savory dishes and bread.

Read Isaiah 28:23-29 to discover a biblical gardening lesson alongside a life lesson.

"Listen and hear my voice; pay attention and hear what I say. When a farmer plows for planting, does he plow continually? Does he keep on breaking up and working the soil? When he has leveled the surface, does he not sow caraway and scatter cumin? Does he not plant wheat in its place, barley in its plot, and spelt in its field? His God instructs him and teaches him the right way. Caraway is not threshed with a sledge, nor is the wheel of a cart rolled over cumin; caraway is beaten out with a rod, and cumin with a stick. Grain must be ground to make bread; so one does not go on threshing it forever. The wheels of a threshing cart may be rolled over it, but one does not use horses to grind grain. All this also comes from the Lord Almighty, whose plan is wonderful, whose wisdom is magnificent."

This passage in Isaiah reminds us of what King Solomon wrote in Ecclesiastes 3:1: "There is a time for everything, and a season for every activity under the heavens."

Pray to God today. Ask God what your life should be producing right now. What are the good and useful seeds you should plant in your life? What things should you learn? What helpful things might you do?

God has a special plan for your life. Trust His all-knowing wisdom.

Jonah's Leafy Plant: Lessons in Gentleness and Mercy

The small book of Jonah contains four action-packed chapters. Let's dig deep into the book of Jonah to discover how God used a leafy plant to guide Jonah on his journey to know God.

The story of Jonah begins when God announced that He had a job for him. But instead of obeying God, Jonah ran away. He hid on a ship that was taking him the opposite direction from where God had told him to go. So to get Jonah's attention God sent a great storm that tossed the boat so violently that the sailors feared they would drown. Jonah knew the storm was his fault and told the sailors to throw him overboard. At first they said no, but at last they were so desperate that they tossed him overboard into the wild waves. At that, the storm stopped, and the sailors immediately found faith in God.

But God didn't give up on Jonah.

God ordered a huge fish to swallow Jonah and keep him in its belly for three days and nights. Jonah came to his senses, prayed desperately, and God let the fish spit out Jonah on a beach. Back on dry land, Jonah decided it was time for him to do what God had told him to do, so he made the long trip to Nineveh and delivered God's message of destruction to the people living there.

The Ninevite king believed Jonah and ordered his people to change their ways. When God saw that the Ninevites' change of heart was true, He showed them mercy and changed His plan to destroy them. But that made Jonah mad. He was embarrassed that he had told everyone that God was going to destroy them, only to have God change His mind.

Jonah went to the east of Nineveh and plopped down in the dust under a blazing hot sun. God quickly grew a tall leafy plant to give Jonah shade, and Jonah was happy with the plant until God sent a worm to eat it.

Read Jonah 4:9-11, then think about this. God uses the image of the plant's quick destruction to explain why the men and women and boys and girls of Nineveh are worth saving. In the story of Jonah, God is gentle with the sailors, the Ninevites, and Jonah. God demonstrates His belief in Jonah and gently guides Jonah back on the right path.

Is God urging you toward a new path? Change can be scary, but we can do all things with God on our side. Today, invite God to help you be the best you can be.

Modern-Day Miracles

The prayer plant is a houseplant that can inspire daily prayer time, and the obedient plant is an outdoor garden plant that displays a concrete example of living like Jesus. Let's take a close-up view of these green treasures.

The Prayer Plant

If you were to visit a Brazilian rain forest, you might see a plant do an amazing "trick." Every night the leaves of the prayer plant rise up and fold together like praying hands.

In the humid forest a hard rain pelts the towering trees overhead. A canopy of leaves sifts the rainwater, and it falls on a low-growing, lime-green plant at your feet. Fat droplets rest on the flat, oval leaves of the prayer plant.

As the plant raises its leaves, the raindrops wash down the stem and soak the roots. Some botanists believe the prayer plant raises its leaves to conserve this moisture. If the prayer plant did not lift its leaves, the water might simply evaporate. By lifting its leaves as if in prayer, the prayer plant waters its own roots and helps the entire forest stay humid.

Since the prayer plant folds its leaves upward only at nighttime, other botanists believe the plant folds its leaves to protect itself during the night, perhaps to conserve heat after the sun goes down in the forest. Even though we do not know exactly why the prayer plant raises its leaves at night, it seems to be doing as God intended. It keeps itself and the forest healthy.

Like the prayer plant, we keep ourselves spiritually healthy when we pray. The Bible tells us to "rejoice always, pray continually, give thanks in all circumstances; for this is God's will for you in Christ Jesus" (1 Thess. 5:16-18).

When you pray, talk to God as you would to your best friend. As you pray, think about your day. What good things happened? Thank God for each one. Did anything happen during the day that worried or upset you? Tell God about it. His help may eventually change the problem or simply give you peace by taking away your worry.

Spending time praying to God and listening for His answers allows God's love to soak into our hearts. Prayer keeps us healthy, inside out, like the rainwater that washes down the prayer plant's upturned leaves and nourishes its roots in the Brazilian rain forest. Prayer plants have become popular houseplants, and many people say the plant reminds them to pray.

Jesus' Prayer

Look up John 17 and be blessed by reading the longest prayer of Jesus recorded in the Scriptures. Jesus prays about His mission as the Son of God. "Now this is eternal life: that they know you, the only true God, and Jesus Christ, whom you have sent. I have brought you glory on earth by finishing the work you gave me to do. And now, Father, glorify me in your presence with the glory I had with you before the world began," He said (verses 3-5).

Jesus then spends the next moments eloquently and earnestly praying for His disciples. "My prayer is not that you take them out of the world," Jesus prays, "but that you protect them from the evil one. They are not of the world, even as I am not of it. Sanctify them by the truth; your word is truth. As you sent me into the world, I have sent them into the world. For them I sanctify myself, that they too may be truly sanctified" (verses 15-19).

Last, Jesus extends His prayer to include all of His followers down through history:

"My prayer is not for them alone. I pray also for those who will believe in me through their message, that all of them may be one, Father, just as you are in me and I am in you. . . . I have made you known to them, and will continue to make you known in order that the love you have for me may be in them and that I myself may be in them" (verses 20-26).

Isn't it wonderful that throughout His own prayer for Himself, His disciples, and all followers, Jesus makes promises by pledging to protect us, guide us, and sanctify us? And take heart; Jesus always keeps His promises! His every move is not for Himself but for us.

An Obedient Plant

Read Luke 2:41-52. When Jesus was 12 years old, He and His parents likely traveled from Nazareth to Jerusalem with a large group of family and friends to celebrate the Festival of the Passover. This holiday commemorated God's act of "passing over" the Israelites' homes (which bore the protective visible mark of blood of a sacrificial lamb on the doorpost), thus sparing them from the last of the 10 plagues that God inflicted against the Egyptians in an effort to free the Israelites from slavery.

When the festival ended, the Galilean caravan departed north toward Nazareth with women and children in front and a group of men walking behind. At age 12, in that society Jesus was considered to be on a threshold between childhood and adulthood. Mary likely thought Jesus was with the men, while Joseph likely thought that He was with the women and children. It was only after a full day's travel that they realized Jesus was missing. Frantic, they turned to hurry back to Jerusalem and searched for their son for three days.

At last they found Jesus in the Temple in deep, calm discussion with the spiritual leaders. The Bible tells us that when His anxious mother chided Him for worrying her, Jesus asked, " 'Why were you searching for me? Didn't you know I had to be in my Father's house?' But they did not understand what he was saying to them. Then he went down to Nazareth with them and was obedient to them. But his mother treasured all these things in her heart. And Jesus grew in wisdom and stature, and in favor with God and man" (Luke 2:49-52).

In the garden obedient plants sometimes grow five feet tall. The white or lavender flower stalks grow vertically, but if you bend them into a horizontal position, they stay put. Hence, gardeners give this plant the common name "obedient plant." An obedient plant is a perennial garden plant, meaning it will return every year. During the cold of winter the plant's green stalks and leaves die off, but in spring the plant grows back from the root system. The blossoms of an obedient plant also drop seeds that form new plants.

As Jesus neared the end of His earthly life, He knew that His most difficult challenge was yet to come. After celebrating the Last Supper with His disciples, again during the Passover in Jerusalem, He went to the Garden of Gethsemane, which is at the foot of the Mount of Olives, to pray. Luke 22:41, 42 records Jesus' obedience to His Father's plan: "He withdrew about a stone's throw beyond them, knelt down and prayed, 'Father, if you are willing, take this cup from me; yet not my will, but yours be done.'"

Sometimes obedience seems like hard work. We'd rather have our own way, but we can ask, as Jesus did in the Garden of Gethsemane, for God's guidance and will to be done.

Prayer Focus

Dear God, thank You for all the green lessons we find in the Bible and all the green things that grow on earth. Thank You for giving us green things to eat that help our bodies stay strong and healthy. Give us confidence in Your plans for us and help us to live joyful, prayerful, obedient lives. Amen.

Zoom Lens

Read John 19:38-42. How many pounds of aloes and myrrh did Joseph of Arimathea and Nicodemus use to prepare the body of Jesus for burial? Today many people still use aloe vera to relieve sunburn and help heal small cuts.

Action Shot

Bake a minty treat—peppermint brownies—for someone special.

In a large bowl, mix by hand: 1 cup melted butter, 6 tablespoons cocoa, and 1 cup sugar. Add 4 eggs, 2 cups flour, and 1 or 2 drops peppermint extract (depending on your taste). Mix and pour into a greased 9" x 13" pan. Bake at 350°F for 30 minutes. Cool, cut into squares, and enjoy.

Section Two

Tasty Tales: Bread, Fruit, and Honey

Taste and see that the Lord is good.
—Psalm 34:8

Chapter 5

Daily Bread: Living in the Moment

Keep falsehood and lies far from me;
give me neither poverty nor riches,
but give me only my daily bread.
—Proverbs 30:8

You or your parents may stop by the grocery store to pick up your daily bread, but in Bible times farmers and their families grew their own crops of grain to make bread. Seeds, those miraculous living things, produce grain that is harvested, ground into flour, mixed with water and yeast, and kneaded into a loaf of bread. The scent of fresh bread baking in an oven says, "Welcome! Comfort is at hand."

A supreme comfort food, bread is also a symbol of life. Dubbed the staff of life, bread *gives* life to those who eat it. A loaf of bread meets our basic physical needs, while Jesus, "the Bread of Life," fulfills our spiritual needs.

Psalm 147:14 proclaims bread a symbol of peace: "He grants peace to your borders and satisfies you with the finest of wheat"; and Psalm 78:24, 25 reminds us that God always provides as He did for Moses and His people in the wilderness: "He rained down manna for the people to eat, he gave them the grain of heaven. Human beings ate the bread of angels; he sent them all the food they could eat." When God delivered the people into the Holy Land, He promised "a land where bread will not be scarce and you will lack nothing" (Deut. 8:9).

Read the story of Jesus' birth in Luke 2:4-7. Now read John 7:42. Which Old Testament king was also born in Bethlehem?

In the Hebrew language *Bethlehem* means "house of bread." Let's walk through the grain fields with other Bible characters as we give thanks that God always provides our daily bread.

The Kindness of Boaz

In Ruth 2 we see the widow Ruth gathering leftover barley from Boaz's fields to help her mother-in-law, Naomi, and herself survive. Boaz was following God's command to help the poor: "When you reap the harvest of your land, do not reap to the very edges of your field or gather the gleanings of your harvest. Leave them for the poor and for the foreigner residing among you. I am the Lord your God" (Lev. 23:22). Boaz showed extraordinary kindness by instructing his workers to intentionally drop extra barley for Ruth to pick up.

The Bottomless Jars

Read 1 Kings 17:7-16 and visualize the widow in the story. Though her land was in a severe drought, she diligently went about her daily duties. But sadly, she was preparing to bake the last bread she would ever eat! When the prophet Elijah asked her to share her small meal with him, she said, "I don't have any bread—only a handful of flour in a jar and a little olive oil in a jug. I am gathering a few sticks to take home and make a meal for myself and my son, that we may eat it—and die" (verse 12).

Hearing that, Elijah promised her that if she would bring him a piece of bread, she would always have enough bread and oil—each day—for herself, her son, and for Elijah. "The jar of flour will not be used up and the jug of oil will not run dry until the day the Lord sends rain on the land," he told her (verse 14). The woman did as Elijah asked, and God provided for their needs, refilling the flour and oil jars each day.

The widow in this story is an example of the "plain, common work" that Scottish author Robert Louis Stevenson is said to have written about: "The best things in life are nearest: breath in your nostrils, light in your eyes, flowers at your feet, duties at your hand, the path of right just before you. Then do not grasp at the stars, but do life's plain, common work as it comes, certain that daily duties and daily bread are the sweetest things in life."

The widow took the "path of right," and God provided.

What do you need from God today?

Just as the widow trusted the words of God's prophet, trust in God's ability to provide for your needs.

Bread of Life

In John 6:9 Jesus' followers saw Him feed 5,000 people with five barley loaves and two small fish. Like the widow whose flour and oil never ran out, Jesus supplied the daily needs of His followers through the bottomless supply in the baskets of bread and fish. Afterward, in amazement, His disciples gathered up 12 baskets of leftovers. The next day the crowds again found Jesus and asked Him how *they* could do God's work.

Jesus answered: "The work of God is this: to believe in the one he has sent" (John 6:29). The people then asked for a sign from Jesus, similar to the manna sent from heaven to Moses and his people.

Jesus explained that the Father gives true bread from heaven. "For the bread of God is the bread that comes down from heaven and gives life to the world," He said (John 6:33). Hearing this, the people told Him that they always want this bread. "Then Jesus declared, 'I am the bread of life. Whoever comes to me will never go hungry, and whoever believes in me will never be thirsty'" (verse 35). Jesus understands that we need earthly bread to sustain our bodies, but He invites us into a relationship with Him to sustain our spirits.

Walking With Jesus

It was likely early summer when Jesus and His disciples walked through the field of soft, ripe grain in Luke 6. "One Sabbath Jesus was going through the grainfields, and his disciples began to pick some heads of grain, rub them in their hands and eat the kernels" (verse 1). The Pharisees asked Jesus, "Why are you doing what is unlawful on the Sabbath?" (verse 2). The Pharisees were strict about following the Law, but Jesus wanted to teach people the deeper meaning of God's love and His will for each person. Jesus' answer to them was "Have you never read what David did when he and his companions were hungry? He entered the house of God, and taking the consecrated bread, he ate what is lawful only for priests to eat. And he also gave some to his companions. . . . The Son of Man is Lord of the Sabbath" (verses 3-5).

Read 1 Samuel 21:4-6 to hear the story of David's desperate need for bread that Jesus spoke of in the previous text. Both David and Jesus set an example that human need sometimes takes precedence over rules. Jesus reminds us that God cares for the simple, everyday needs of His children and will provide. New grains, such as those the disciples picked, were sometimes toasted over an open fire before being eaten. "If you bring a grain offering of firstfruits to the Lord, offer crushed heads of new grain roasted in the fire" (Lev. 2:14).

Prayer Lessons

We know that Jesus hears us no matter how we pray, but sometimes we want to be sure that we're asking for our daily bread in a respectful way. To put our fears to rest, Jesus gave us several prayer lessons. Matthew 6:6 says: "When you pray, go into your room, close the door and pray to your Father, who is unseen. Then your Father, who sees what is done in secret, will reward you."

Jesus also says: "Your Father knows what you need before you ask him. This, then, is how you should pray: 'Our Father in heaven, hallowed be your name, your kingdom come, your will be done, on earth as it is in heaven. Give us today our daily bread. And forgive us our debts, as we also have forgiven our debtors. And lead us not into temptation, but deliver us from the evil one'" (verses 8-13).

The Lord's Prayer gives us a pattern for prayer. Jesus says we should show gratitude for God and ask God to help us do what He wants us to do. We should tell God our needs and concerns and then trust in His answers.

When we pray, we can also tell God what is truly on our hearts. Read this encouraging promise: "Ask and it will be given to you; seek and you will find; knock and the door will be opened to you" (Luke 11:9).

Find a quiet, private moment today and talk to God as your best friend.

Bubbles Below the Surface

Read the parable of the yeast and flour in Matthew 13:33. Can you imagine God's kingdom as being similar to a housewife making bread? When the woman works yeast into the dough, it bubbles and froths, making the flour expand and rise. Maybe your mom, or even you, have made yeast bread as this verse describes—adding the yeast and sweetener to liquid, then stirring in the flour. When the dough rises to just the right size, it can be baked into a delicious treat. In a way similar to the silent growth of yeast, God often works silently in our hearts, below the surface of life's situations, and in places we can't see.

Harvesting Peace

Read the parable of the wheat and weeds in Matthew 13:24-30 and Jesus' explanation of it in verses 36 to 43. Jesus used images that were familiar to His listeners to make His lessons come alive. The people who heard this story often walked through fields of wheat. They understood the necessity of weeding their crops and separating weeds from the grain at harvest time. Jesus' parable helps us see that judgment is best left in God's hands. When we see wrongs in our world, we often want to see them made right. Sometimes that's not possible. Only God is capable of understanding all sides of every situation—past, present, and future. When we judge others, we place a heavy, unnecessary burden on ourselves. Leaving that burden in God's hands helps us find our peace.

The Last Supper

Recorded in Matthew 26 is the last supper that Jesus and His disciples shared together before the Crucifixion. During that special meal Jesus "took bread, and when he had given thanks, he broke it and gave it to his disciples, saying, 'Take and eat; this is my body'" (verse 26). Jesus' act of breaking and sharing bread with His friends figuratively represented His sacrifice—His life and death in our place; bread, therefore, becomes the symbol of eternal life, the greatest gift from God to humankind.

Celebrating the Lord's Supper allows us to honor and remember Jesus' last meal with His disciples, to thank Jesus for His work in our hearts and minds, to commune with other followers, and to draw closer to God.

Prayer Focus

Dear God, thank You for the gift of life and for providing our daily bread in every way, every day. Help us to reap the lessons You have in store for us today. Thank You for Jesus' life. Help us to follow Him with gratitude, accepting Him as the Bread of Life and the source of everlasting peace. Amen.

Zoom Lens

When God delivered the Israelites from Egypt, He provided for all their needs. Exodus 16 tells us that six days a week God sent a flaky substance from heaven so the Israelites could make bread. The Israelites did not know what the gift from heaven was, so they called it "manna," which in Hebrew means "What is it?" Read Exodus 16:35 to discover how many years the Lord provided manna to the Israelites "until they reached the border of Canaan."

Action Shot

Take a walk through a park or field and imagine you are walking with Jesus through a field of fresh grain. Ask Him any questions you have. Ask Him for your daily bread.

Jesus reminds us to take life one day at a time. He said, "Do not worry about tomorrow, for tomorrow will worry about itself. Each day has enough trouble of its own" (Matt. 6:34). When we walk beside Jesus, we have no reason to worry. All is well. Take your day one moment at a time, asking Jesus to make your path straight.

Chapter 6

Fruit: A Spiritual Harvest

God blessed them and said to them, "Be fruitful."
—Genesis 1:28

Walk with the Israelites out of Egypt, a land where some winters passed with little or no rain, a land where farmers irrigated their fields with water from the Nile River. Cross the Red Sea. Hear Moses' promise: "For the Lord your God is bringing you into a good land—a land with brooks, streams, and deep springs gushing out into the valleys and hills; a land with wheat and barley, vines and fig trees, pomegranates, olive oil and honey" (Deut. 8:7, 8).

Moses' description of the seven foods—wheat, barley, grapes, figs, pomegranates, olives, and honey—makes the Promised Land sound like a Garden of Eden. When Moses sent 12 spies to scout out the land, they brought back abundant fruits, likely figs, grapes, and pomegranates (Num. 13:26, 27).

Today when you visit a local farmer's market or fruit stand, you're rewarded with the same visual paradise. The glorious array of fruits of different sizes, shapes, and colors inspire us to say a silent "Thank you" to the farmers who cultivate, care for, and harvest fruit from the earth's trees, vines, and plants.

Each fruit contains a seed—or seeds—that can grow into another tree, vine, or plant that bears more fruit. A Welsh proverb says, "A seed hidden in the heart of an apple is an orchard invisible."

Fruits give us fresh seeds of hope; they symbolize abundance and the notion that life can constantly start anew. As Isaiah 65:8 says: "When juice is still found in a cluster of grapes . . . , 'Don't destroy it, there is still a blessing in it.' "

The Bible's fruitful stories include a bountiful harvest of spiritual lessons. For example, 1 Kings 4:25 marks fruit as a symbol of peace: "During Solomon's lifetime Judah and Israel, from Dan to Beersheba, lived in safety, everyone under their own vine and under their own fig tree."

Like most fruits, the fruit of the fig tree is "good and sweet" (Judges 9:11).

Read 2 Chronicles 3:16. Which fruit inspired some of King Solomon's decorations in the Temple of the Lord?

Let's harvest other wholesome, fruitful stories from the Bible.

Cluster of Grapes: The Nine

Jesus sets the parable of the two sons in a grape vineyard to show us the power of obedience. Read Matthew 21:28-32. Will you be like the first or second son? Jesus reminds us to hear God's call and follow through by harvesting good fruit in our lives.

Scripture tells us there are nine parts to the fruit of the Holy Spirit: "The fruit of the Spirit is love, joy, peace, patience, kindness, goodness, faithfulness, gentleness, self-control; against such things there is no law" (Gal. 5:22, 23, NASB). The nine facets of the fruit of the Spirit are like a cluster of grapes all clinging to one stem. It offers us a beautiful picture of how to live like Jesus.

Let's study Bible characters who display the fruit of the Spirit by their example. They help us consider the essence of things, the core of the matter.

Love Rules

Love, a gift offered freely, is part of our inheritance as children of God. Read 1 Corinthians 13 to remind yourself of the definition of love. Love is the need to give and receive affection. We cannot prosper without love, but we can be sure of God's love for us and that He will help us love others.

One time a Pharisee and expert in the law asked Jesus, "'Teacher, which is the greatest commandment in the Law?' Jesus replied: 'Love the Lord your God with all your heart and with all your soul and with all your mind.' This is the first and greatest commandment. And the second is like it: 'Love your neighbor as yourself.' All the Law and the Prophets hang on these two commandments" (Matt. 22:36-40).

The "Law and the Prophets" Jesus spoke of refers to the *Torah* (a Hebrew word that means *the Law*), which consists of (1) the five books of Moses (Genesis, Exodus, Leviticus, Numbers, and Deuteronomy); and (2) the *Nevi'im* (the Prophets), which includes the former prophets (Joshua, Judges, Samuel, and Kings), the latter prophets (Isaiah, Jeremiah, and Ezekiel), and the 12 minor prophets (Hosea, Joel, Amos, Obadiah, Jonah, Micah, Nahum, Habakkuk, Zephaniah, Haggai, Zechariah, and Malachi).

Jesus reminds us that we need to remember only two rules regarding love, and He used Old Testament Scripture to explain it: "Love the Lord your God with all your heart and with all your soul and with all your strength" (Deut. 6:5), and "love your neighbor as yourself" (Lev. 19:18). The collective wisdom of the Law and the

Prophets is summed up in Jesus' two simple rules: Love God. Love others.

Jesus' four little words have the power to make a huge difference in our world. Let's put Jesus' words into action today.

The Disciples' Joy

Joy is absolute delight, pleasure, and elation. Read Luke 24. Put yourself in the sandals of a disciple who has just heard that Jesus has been raised from the dead! Do you feel that same joy today? Luke 24:52, 53 describes the disciples' reaction after they touch the risen Jesus, share a meal with Him, hear Him teach, and watch Him ascend to heaven: "They worshiped him and returned to Jerusalem with great joy. And they stayed continually at the temple, praising God."

As the disciples and their friends joined together to share Jesus' teachings with everyone they met, they echoed King Solomon's reminder from Ecclesiastes 4:9 that the followers of God should join in partnerships: "Two are better than one." And Jesus reaffirms this, saying, "For where two or three gather in my name, there am I with them" (Matt. 18:20).

Today, find someone to share your joy with!

Hannah's Peace

If you were a woman living in Bible times, one of the most important things you could do was to have children. And not just one or two children, but many, many children. The more the better!

The first chapter of 1 Samuel tells the story of Hannah, a married woman who did not have any children. Day after day—and then year after year—she prayed that God would bless her with a baby. When she saw other women with all their children, she thought that her heart would break. She felt especially troubled because when a woman back then couldn't have children, people thought she was being punished by God.

Every year Hannah and her husband took a long trip to go to the tabernacle. This was a very special church for special worship. And one year Hannah decided to take her sorrow to God in a very special way. Through her tearful prayer, Hannah made peace with God. Then she told God that if He granted her deepest wish for a baby boy, she would give the child back to Him.

God said yes to her prayer. Soon after Hannah returned home she realized that she was going to have a baby. Try to imagine how happy this made Hannah! She was finally going to be a mother. At last she had peace.

When the baby boy was born, she named him Samuel, which means "name of God." Now, remember that Hannah had promised God that if He would send her a son, she would give that son back to Him. When Samuel was just a few years old, Hannah knew it was time for her to keep her promise.

Once again Hannah showed the fruit of peace. This story shows us the strength that God's peace brings, for on their yearly visit to the tabernacle Hannah gave little Samuel to Priest Eli. She left him there to fulfill her promise to God. Samuel would have a new life in God's house.

In 1 Samuel 1:28 we see a wise definition of *peace* in Hannah's words: "Now I give him to the Lord. For his whole life he will be given over to the Lord." It is our privilege to give things, both good and bad, to the Lord. We can surrender God's blessings back to Him by showing gratitude for His goodness. We can surrender anything that bothers us by inviting God to transform our minds.

What do you need to give to God today? Can you thank God for a specific blessing in your life? Is there any area of your life that you can invite God's transforming power?

A Patient Gardener

In Luke 13:6-9, read Jesus' parable about a barren tree that has not produced fruit for three years. The owner of the barren fig tree is a straightforward businessman. He logically concludes that if the tree isn't making figs for him to sell, he should have the gardener of the vineyard cut it down. But the gardener who has been trimming and fertilizing the fig tree is very patient with the tree, so he pleads with the owner to give it just one more year. He believes in the tree as much as God believes in you and me. In the same way that he asked the owner to let the tree live one more year and see if it begins to bear fruit, our patient God gives us the chance to try again, and again, and again.

Are there any opportunities that you've missed in life? Are there any mistakes you'd like to correct? Today is your day to try again.

The Kind Landowner

Matthew 20:1-16 tells the parable of the workers in the vineyard. The landowner hired workers early, at 9:00 a.m. Then he hired more workers at noon, then at 3:00 p.m., and at 5:00 p.m. When the workday ended, he paid all the workers the same amount of money—those who had worked since early morning and those who didn't start working until late in the afternoon.

Those who had worked all day were disappointed that they didn't earn more than the workers who started later, and they were very unhappy that the late workers were paid the same amount of money they were. But the landowner told them, "I am not being unfair to you, friend. . . . Don't I have the right to do what I want with my own money?" (Matt. 20:13-15).

This story gives us an example of how to treat others each day of our lives. Kindness is the compassionate, considerate, helpful treatment of others. When we are able to help others, we should.

On a deeper level Jesus' parable offers us a glimpse of God's kindness. God's grace doesn't have to be earned and is freely given to everyone who claims their faith in Jesus, no matter how young or old they are when they do so. We're faithful to a God of mercy. Jesus also assures us that we don't need to have all the answers and that some questions are best left in God's hands.

Zechariah and Elizabeth's Goodness

Examine the goodness Zechariah and Elizabeth showed in Luke 1:5-25. Goodness is virtuous, honorable, worthy behavior. Zechariah and Elizabeth's goodness was rewarded by the Lord's goodness. What fruit did their goodness bear? Psalm 107:1 reminds us, "Give thanks to the Lord, for he is good; his love endures forever."

Ruth's Faithfulness

Do you remember the story of Ruth and Naomi? Naomi and her husband and two sons had moved to a foreign land because there was no food in their homeland. Several years later, after Naomi's husband and two sons died, she decided to go back home.

Ruth had been married to one of Naomi's sons, but now he was dead. Ruth walked with her mother-in-law, Naomi, to the end of the village, and now it was time for them to say goodbye. But Ruth could not stand to let Naomi go.

Ruth's words to Naomi are a good definition of faithfulness. This is what she said: "Where you go I will go, and where you stay I will stay. Your people will be my people and your God my God" (Ruth 1:16).

Ruth gave her loyalty, confidence, trust, and allegiance to Naomi. Chapter 3 of the book of Ruth shows Ruth's utter faithfulness to Naomi. With complete trust and abandon, Ruth followed Naomi's instructions exactly, which led to Ruth's marriage to Boaz. And in Ruth 4:14-17 we learn that Ruth became the great-grandmother of King David, who was an ancestor of Jesus. Read Matthew 1:1-17 to learn the full genealogy from Abraham to David to Jesus.

At first glance the book of Ruth is a heartwarming story about a young widow's hard times turned to blessing. Ruth followed her heart when she refused to let Naomi go back to her homeland without her. Ruth was faithful because she knew it was the right thing to do in those circumstances. Ruth didn't know that God had a huge purpose for her life, but God extended the fruits of her faithfulness far beyond her lifetime.

Find one small way to be faithful to God today and trust His plan for the results, even if you never do learn the outcome.

Jesus' Gentle Words

One day Jesus visited the home of Martha and Mary in Bethany, just outside Jerusalem. Like many women in Bible times, Martha had to work hard every day to finish all her household chores. Martha was preoccupied with cooking a nice meal for Jesus and His friends, but her sister, Mary, settled herself on the floor right in front, near Jesus' feet. Mary's only aim was to hear Jesus teach.

As Martha worked in the kitchen she got hotter and hotter and madder and madder because she was doing all the work. So Martha went to Jesus and asked Him to tell Mary to come help. Instead of doing that, Jesus gently calmed and comforted Martha. He politely told her that Mary's choice to put God's teachings first in her life was the right decision. Jesus would be content with a simple meal so that Martha could spend time with Him, too. See Luke 10:38-42.

Are you more of a Martha or a Mary?

While Mary's devotion to Jesus is a good thing, Martha also spent her time in a commendable way—serving others. She wanted the meal to be perfect for Jesus and His friends. Jesus understood Martha's need to accomplish her daily work, but He gently asked her to set priorities. Are there times when you are too busy doing your schoolwork or helping your friends that you don't take time to simply sit at Jesus' feet?

Life is a constant balancing act; be gentle with yourself. Today, spend time helping others, serving others, *and* spend a few moments simply sitting still in God's presence.

Abigail's Self-control

Read 1 Samuel 25:2-44 to hear how Abigail used self-control to save her household. Self-control is restraint; it is the ability to see beyond what you need right now in order to grasp the big picture. Abigail's husband Nabal did not see the big picture. He refused David's request for food, even though David had been good and helpful to Nabal's men.

When Abigail heard that Nabal offended David, she took matters into her own hands. Abigail packed up a lot of food to take to David. It was enough food to feed a small army and included 200 loaves of bread, parched grain, 100 clusters of raisins, and 200 fig cakes. As Abigail rode her donkey to deliver all this food, she met David and his soldiers. They were on their way to fight! Abigail's self-controlled speech and her grasp of the big picture stopped David from killing Nabal. And David was so impressed with Abigail that, after Nabal died, David asked her to marry him.

The next time a difficult situation arises, remember Abigail and ask God to enable you to see the big picture.

Prayer Focus

Dear God, thank You for the healthy, sweet gift of fruits. Thank You for the stories of the Bible's many characters who guide us toward living a glorious, abundant, Spirit-filled life. Show us the fruits of the Spirit that You want us to cultivate and harvest in our own lives today. Amen.

Zoom Lens

Read Genesis 2:17. When God planted the first garden, He told Adam to avoid the fruit of only one tree. No one knows what the tree of the knowledge of good and evil actually looked like, though in paintings it is often depicted as an apple tree. But it could have been a kind of tree that we don't even know about.

How do you visualize the forbidden fruit in the Garden of Eden? Take a moment to ask God if there are fruits—or bad habits—in your life that you should avoid.

Action Shot

If you or your parents have a garden or trees in the yard, take a stroll and find a plant or tree that needs pruning. Take along your Bible and read John 15:1-4 in which Jesus likens Himself to a grapevine and God as the gardener. Caring for a plant can remind us to care for ourselves. As you prune your garden plant into a more desirable shape, ask Jesus if there are areas in your life that should be pruned away. Pruning is almost always helpful to a plant and usually results in it bearing more fruit. Expect Jesus' work in your life to make you a stronger, healthier, and more fruitful member of God's family. Jesus tells us, "I chose you and appointed you so that you might go and bear fruit—fruit that will last—and so that whatever you ask in my name the Father will give you. This is my command: Love each other" (John 15:16, 17).

Chapter 7

Honey: Sweet Stories

[God and his laws] are more precious than gold, than much pure gold; they are sweeter than honey, than honey from the honeycomb.
—Psalm 19:10

King David had great respect for God, His laws, and one of nature's sweetest foods—honey. God designed bees in a truly amazing way to share this special gift with us.

This spring and summer look closely at the flowers and trees that are in bloom. You may see a bee buzzing above the blossoms, collecting pollen and nectar. Bees have long tongues like straws to suck the nectar out of flowers. Bees store nectar in their stomachs for about half an hour, where it is transformed into honey. Back at the hive, the bees regurgitate the honey into beeswax combs, fan their wings to dry the honey, and cover the filled honeycomb with wax.

In *The Healthy Taste of Honey: Bee People's Recipes, Anecdotes, and Lore*, author Larry Lonik writes, "Honeybees are the most pleasant, sociable, genial, and good-natured little beings that can be encountered in all animated creation—when they are understood."

Honeybees fly 55,000 miles and visit 2 million flowers to make one pound of honey. We are lucky that bees make enough honey to share and that beekeepers collect the excess honey so that we all can have honey to eat. Examining the gift of honey can inspire kindness and generosity in our own character. Human beings can work together for good as bees do.

Some biblical scholars believe the honey mentioned in the seven food species of Deuteronomy 8:8—"wheat and barley, vines and fig trees, pomegranates, olive oil and honey"—was actually a fruit. The "honey" in the Promised Land may have been the juice of date fruits from the date palm tree. Whatever the case, other Bible verses refer to bees making honey. Read Judges 14:8, 9 to hear of a time Samson found bees and honey.

Read Genesis 43:11. What sweet treat does this verse suggest as a gift? Let's look at some other sweet stories that are drizzled throughout the Bible.

A Voice in the Wilderness

Many Bible stories tell about God's people using honey as food. John the Baptist, son of Zechariah and Elizabeth, was the prophet who prepared the way for Jesus to come and share His message.

Isaiah 40:3 prophesied John's arrival: "A voice of one calling: 'In the wilderness prepare the way for the Lord; make straight in the desert a highway for our God.'" Matthew 3:1-3 repeats Isaiah's words: "In those days John the Baptist came, preaching in the wilderness of Judea and saying, 'Repent, for the kingdom of heaven has come near.' This is he who was spoken of through the prophet Isaiah: 'A voice of one calling in the wilderness, "Prepare the way for the Lord, make straight paths for him."'"

The following is how Mark 1:6 describes John the Baptist living in the wilderness: "John wore clothing made of camel's hair, with a leather belt around his waist, and he ate locusts and wild honey." Matthew 3 and Mark 1 are treasure troves of colorful stories about John. They bring to mind a wild-eyed, bushy-haired man living rough on the open desert, perhaps with sprigs of wild herbs tucked in his belt. John reminds us a bit of the outspoken Old Testament prophet Elijah, who also lived off the land near the Jordan River (1 Kings 17:2-6).

People traveled from far and wide to see John, hear him preach, and to be baptized by him in the Jordan River. John told his followers, "I baptize you with water for repentance. But after me comes one who is more powerful than I, whose sandals I am not worthy to carry. He will baptize you with the Holy Spirit and fire" (Matt. 3:11).

Food for Thought

When you eat honey, think of John the Baptist, the coarsely dressed prophet whom God chose to baptize Jesus (verse 13; Mark 1:9) and point the way toward Jesus.

Lonik says that each American consumes 60 to 120 pounds of refined sugar every year. Since white sugar contains no nutritional value, the nutritional powerhouse of honey is a substitute worth considering in many recipes. Honey is 25 to 50 percent sweeter than sugar, so adjust your recipe to fit your sweet tooth. Proverbs 25:16 reminds us to exercise moderation in all that we do: "If you find honey, eat just enough—too much of it, and you will vomit."

One of nature's perfect foods, honey is packed with antioxidants, essential amino acids (the building blocks for protein), vitamins, and minerals. Honey sweetens up a fruit smoothie or a cup of tea, but your favorite way to eat honey may be right off the spoon.

Psalm 119:103 praises God this way: "How sweet are your words to my taste, sweeter than honey to my mouth!"

The God of Rescue

When the children of Israel lived in slavery in Egypt for hundreds of years, they were terribly mistreated and forced to work in horrible conditions. But God had a rescue plan for them. He told Moses, "I have come down to rescue them from the hand of the Egyptians and to bring them up out of that land into a good and spacious land, a land flowing with milk and honey" (Ex. 3:8).

But Moses was reluctant to follow God's orders. He was afraid the people of Israel would not believe that he truly was God's messenger. God convinced Moses to get up out of his fear, and with God's help Moses was able to lead the children of Israel to safety. After they had been enslaved in Egypt for so many years, the image of "a land flowing with milk and honey" must have been beautiful to the Israelites. Anytime we go through a hard time, God can raise us up and deliver us out of the problem.

Bread From Heaven, Spices, and Honey

After the Israelites were delivered from Egypt, they had a long journey ahead of them before they could reach that land of milk and honey God had promised them. They traveled through a vast, unfamiliar wilderness and were afraid they would starve, but God never failed to provide for their needs. Each day He sent food from heaven. Exodus 16:14 describes the food as "a flaky substance as fine as frost" (NLT). At first the people did not know what it was, but Moses explained it was bread from God. Exodus 16:31 says, "The people of Israel called the bread manna. It was white like coriander seed and tasted like wafers made with honey."

Prayer Focus

Dear God, thank You for the sweet gift of honey, for honeybees, and most of all for the pearls of wisdom we find in Your words. Help us to work together for good and show kindness to others today. Amen.

Zoom Lens

One morning for breakfast, taste the Israelites' manna. Spread some honey on a slice of breakfast toast. If you wish, mix a dash of crushed coriander seed into the honey. As you nibble your toast, give thanks to God for taking care of all your needs.

Now open your Bible to Proverbs, a book of wisdom filled with lessons on how to live the way God wants us to. Read Proverbs 24:14. What hope do you visualize for your future? Our source of hope is never-ending, like honey in a bee's hive. As the bees continue their daily work, we must also continue ours.

Action Shot

King Solomon wrote, "Gracious words are a honeycomb, sweet to the soul and healing to the bones" (Prov. 16:24). Every time we speak a word to another person, we should try to make those words as sweet as honey.

Think of the different people you see every day. How can you show kindness to each one of them?

At the end of the day, count how many people you spoke kindly to or did an act of kindness for.

Section Three

Wild Things in the Bible: Fish, Birds, Beasts, and Bugs

And God said, "Let the water teem with living creatures,
and let birds fly above the earth across the vault of the sky."
So God created the great creatures of the sea
and every living thing with which the water teems
and that moves about in it, according to their kinds,
and every winged bird according to its kind.
And God saw that it was good. God blessed them and said,
"Be fruitful and increase in number and fill the water in the seas,
and let the birds increase on the earth."
And there was evening, and there was morning—the fifth day.
And God said, "Let the land produce living creatures according to their kinds:
the livestock, the creatures that move along the ground, and the wild animals,
each according to its kind." And it was so.
God made the wild animals according to their kinds,
the livestock according to their kinds,
and all the creatures that move along the ground according to their kinds.
And God saw that it was good.
—Genesis 1:20-25

Chapter 8

Fishy Tales: Goodness and Contentment

Taking the five loaves and the two fish and looking up to heaven, he gave thanks and broke the loaves.
—Matthew 14:19

Gaze out over the blue-green waters of the Sea of Galilee where Jesus focused His three-year ministry. Notice the seaside villages sprawled along the shoreline—Bethsaida, Capernaum, Magdala, and Tiberias. Imagine Jesus walking alongside the shore and calling His first disciples. Jesus "saw two brothers, Simon called Peter and his brother Andrew. They were casting a net into the lake, for they were fishermen. 'Come, follow me,' Jesus said, 'and I will send you out to fish for people' " (Matt. 4:18, 19). As Jesus taught His disciples how to fish for followers, the Bible's stories about fish show us how to fall in line with Jesus' teachings.

Read Matthew 12:40. Find the familiar fish story that Jesus mentions as He foretells His resurrection, saying He will be in the belly of the earth for three days and three nights.

Harp-shaped Lake

The Sea of Galilee is a large freshwater lake fed by the Jordan River and underground springs. It stretches about 13 miles long and eight miles wide. As the Sea of Galilee is situated below sea level and bordered by hills such as Mount Tabor and the Mount of Beatitudes, its climate can change quickly and is subject to abrupt, often fierce, storms. John calls it the Sea of Tiberias (John 6:1), and Luke dubs it Lake of Gennesaret (Luke 5:1). Matthew 4:18 and Mark 1:16 both name it the Sea of Galilee. In the Old Testament the sea was called Sea of Chinnereth, sometimes spelled Kinnereth (Num. 34:11, KJV). *Chinnereth* means "harp" and, therefore, is a fitting name for this harp-shaped lake. The Sea of Galilee remains a prime fishing spot today.

A Sea of Galilee Boat

When Jesus called them to follow Him, Simon Peter and Andrew were likely fishing for sardines, barbels, and tilapia, three edible fish found in the Sea of Galilee. Their small fishing boat may have been crafted from oak, pine, or other timbers from the surrounding woods. It likely resembled the first-century boat discovered along the Sea of Galilee in 1986. Dubbed the "Sea of Galilee Boat," this boat measured 27 feet long by 7.5 feet wide by 4.3 feet high and was crafted from 12 different types of wood. An archaeological team excavated, restored, and preserved the boat for display at the Yigal Alon Museum in the Galilean seaside village of Kibbutz Ginosar (S. Wachamann, *The Sea of Galilee Boat* [1995]).

The Life of a Fisher

Luke 5 shows us that the life of a fisher was not easy. Luke writes of a time when Jesus, after preaching to a large crowd, told Simon Peter to steer his boat toward deep water and cast down the net. Simon Peter's response to Jesus' instructions was "Master, we've worked hard all night and haven't caught anything. But because you say so, I will let down the nets" (verse 5). Again and again, Simon Peter had tossed the heavy net out into the water, waited a while, then pulled the net back in—without success. He was reluctant to throw the cumbersome, heavy net again, for there was no reason to believe throwing that net one more time would make any difference. Yet he cast the net once more—because Jesus asked him to—and the results were staggering! verses 6 and 7 say that they caught so many fish that the nets started to break, they had to call upon their workmates for immediate help, and the boat started to sink.

"When Simon Peter saw this, he fell at Jesus' knees and said, 'Go away from me, Lord; I am a sinful man!' For he and all his companions were astonished at the catch of fish they had taken, and so were James and John, the sons of Zebedee, Simon's partners. Then Jesus said to Simon, 'Don't be afraid; from now on you will fish for people.' So they pulled their boats up on shore, left everything and followed him" (verses 8-11).

Peter and his companions were about to give up because their efforts seemed futile, but when they gave it just one more try under Jesus' guidance, they could hardly contain their catch!

Have you been trying to achieve success in an area of your life again and again without any luck? Have you invited Jesus into the situation?

After Jesus performed this miracle and they hauled in their huge catch of fish, Peter dropped to his knees before Jesus and cried out that he was unworthy. When Jesus reassured him with the words "Don't be afraid," He was saying, "I'll help you cast away the things that need to be cast away like an old, worn-out fishing net. I believe in you. Come with Me."

Jesus says the same to you and me today!

Feeding the Followers

Two unique miracles that Jesus performed—unique because they included *thousands* of people—involve fish. Read "Jesus Feeds the Four Thousand" in Matthew 15:32-39 and Mark 8:1-10. Both accounts say that—among all those people—the disciples were able to find only seven loaves of bread and a few small fish! (And remember, these loaves of bread were not like the larger loaves we usually eat in North America, but small, flat, round loaves that looked more like pita bread.) Matthew adds that Jesus said, "I have compassion for these people; they have already been with me three days and have nothing to eat. I do not want to send them away hungry, or they may collapse on the way" (Matt. 15:32).

Holding the meager supply of fish and bread in His hands, Jesus gave thanks for the food and then began to break it in pieces and give it to His disciples, who were to pass the food out to everyone in this large crowd. And miraculously, every single person there ate until they were full.

Jesus met their basic, physical need simply because He cared about them. After the 4,000 had eaten all that they wanted, the disciples gathered up the leftovers—seven baskets of miracle food.

Now read "Jesus Feeds the Five Thousand" in the four Gospels: Matthew 14:15-21; Mark 6:32-44; Luke 9:10-17; and John 6:1-13. Each Gospel says that the disciples could find only five loaves and two fish, and John adds the detail that the five barley loaves and two fish were a young boy's lunch!

Again Jesus blessed the food, and more than 5,000 were fed and 12 baskets of leftovers remained. Luke provides their exact location, "a town called Bethsaida" (Luke 9:10). A small community on the northeast shore of the Sea of Galilee, Bethsaida is often translated "house of fishing." Bethsaida is home to at least three of Jesus' disciples, Peter, Andrew, and Philip.

John 6:4 tells us the time of year when this happened: "The Jewish Passover Festival was near." On a modern calendar it would be springtime. The grass was green, and possibly trees and flowers were blooming.

Mark tells us that Jesus and His disciples had gone there to be alone for a while, but Jesus had compassion for the crowds of people who followed them there "because they were like sheep without a shepherd. So he began teaching them many things" (Mark 6:34).

When it was time to eat, Jesus told His disciples to "have all the people sit down in groups on the green grass" (verse 39). Mark's version of the story brings to mind the familiar, comforting words of Psalm 23:1, 2: "The Lord is my shepherd, I lack nothing. He makes me lie down in green pastures."

In both stories Jesus is the Good Shepherd tending His flock, ensuring their comfort, and guaranteeing that they lack nothing. Jesus wants us to hear His message of loving God and loving others, but He also wants us to rest assured that He knows our daily needs, even our physical needs, and meets them. In John 14:18 Jesus assures us that He will never stop meeting our needs and will never leave us alone: "I will not leave you comfortless" (KJV). The feeding of the four thousand and of the five thousand shows us that God's love is abundant, there is always enough, and Jesus' devotion to us never wavers.

Teamwork: Fishers and Disciples

Matthew 13:47, 48 contains the parable of the net. Jesus says, "Once again, the kingdom of heaven is like a net that was let down into the lake and caught all kinds of fish. When it was full, the fishermen pulled it up on the shore. Then they sat down and collected the good fish in baskets, but threw the bad away."

The net Jesus mentions in this parable may be a long and heavy dragnet. The disciples would have used their boat to position the dragnet. Pulling in the dragnet required teamwork along with strength and patience. Jesus taught the disciples to work together to do God's work in the same way that the fishers had to work together to pull in their catch. We can ask Jesus to help us "fish out" the good qualities in ourselves and throw away the things in our own character that hold us back from living the life God would have us live.

A Rich Fish: Lessons in Abundance

Read Matthew 17:24-27:

"After Jesus and his disciples arrived in Capernaum, the collectors of the two-drachma temple tax came to Peter and asked, 'Doesn't your teacher pay the temple tax?' 'Yes, he does,' he replied. When Peter came into the house, Jesus was the first to speak. 'What do you think, Simon?' he asked. 'From whom do the kings of the earth collect duty and taxes—from their own children or from others?' 'From others,' Peter answered. 'Then the children are exempt,' Jesus said to him. 'But so that we may not cause offense, go to the lake and throw out your line. Take the first fish you catch; open its mouth and you will find a four-drachma coin. Take it and give it to them for my tax and yours.'"

Matthew, a former tax collector, is the only apostle to include the story of the Temple tax. The tax collectors who asked Peter for the money were following the rule set out in Exodus 30:11-16 to collect atonement money. Each Jewish male over the age of 20 had to pay a Temple tax. The money was used to maintain the Temple.

Do you think Peter was embarrassed that he answered the tax collectors on Jesus' behalf without asking Jesus' opinion first? Do you think Peter was worried that he didn't have the money to pay the tax? In Matthew 8:20 Jesus explained the cost of following Him: "Foxes have dens and birds have nests, but the Son of Man has no place to lay his head." Many of us today cannot imagine living moment to moment as Jesus and His disciples did, but the Bible portrays Jesus living a life of abundance. He believes that everything He needs will come to Him exactly when He needs it. In the story of the Temple tax, four drachma were owed, and Jesus furnished Peter with a four-drachma coin, precisely the amount he needed at the exact moment of need.

King David also believed in abundance; he wrote, "I lack nothing" (Ps. 23:1). Read Exodus 16. During the long years God's people were wandering in the wilderness, God provided manna for them, anew, six days a week. Of course, God told them to gather extra on the sixth day, because manna did not fall on the Sabbath.

Moses tells the people to gather an *omer*, an ancient Israelite unit of measurement equal to about 2.3 quarts, for each person in the tent. Verse 18 says: "When they measured it by the omer, the one who gathered much did not have too much, and the one who gathered little did not have too little. *Everyone had gathered just as much as they needed.*"

Jesus calls His followers to be loyal to Him, the King of heaven and earth. He believes "the children are exempt." Jesus understands, though, that we must live within the rules and parameters of the societies we occupy. Perhaps Jesus chose a fish, a symbol of sustenance, to provide for Peter's need to remind us that God will always sustain us, no matter what our needs. Like Peter, when we prayerfully get up, go out, take the initiative, and do the work, we can reap God's abundance in our own lives.

Prayer Focus

Dear God, thank You for the Bible's illuminating tales about fish. Thank You for the assurance that You care about every small detail of our lives. Give us the courage to ask for help when we need it, and help us to live each day confident that You provide for our every need. Amen.

Zoom Lens

After His death and resurrection, Jesus again used fish to teach His disciples. Read John 21:1-14, a story about a miraculous catch of fish. Imagine the disciples' delight at seeing their Lord and realizing that He continued to provide for their needs. After a long night of fishing, the disciples had not caught a single fish. But then Jesus told them where to place the net, and they brought in a huge haul!

What was the exact number of fish they caught?

Action Shot

Early Christians were persecuted because of their faith and often used the sign of the fish to safely identify themselves to other believers. When two people met, one person would draw a curved line in the sand to make the top part of the fish. If the other person believed in Jesus, he or she would draw a second line to complete the bottom half of the fish. Sit at a computer with another believer and draw a fish using the "less than" and "greater than" keys: <><

If you know someone who doesn't know Jesus, will you be a "fisher of people" today?

Chapter 9

Birds: Songs of Safety and Freedom

He will cover you with his feathers, and under his wings you will find refuge; his faithfulness will be your shield and rampart.
—Psalm 91:4

The Bible uses the majestic characteristics of birds to describe attributes of both God and us, His children. Isaiah 40 speaks of the unsurpassable wisdom, strength, and love of our "everlasting God, the Creator of the ends of the earth," exclaiming that "He will not grow tired or weary" and that "no one can fathom" His understanding (verse 28). It then contrasts His nature to how finite—and needy of Him—we are: "He gives strength to the weary and increases the power of the weak. Even youths grow tired and weary, and young men stumble and fall; but those who hope in the Lord will renew their strength. They will soar on wings like eagles; they will run and not grow weary, they will walk and not be faint" (verses 29-31). And there it is, the beautiful promise that we will "soar on wings like eagles."

What child or grown-up hasn't gazed upon a bird and expressed his or her wish to fly? When you hike a nature trail, a bird's fallen feather is one of the greatest treasures to discover. Birds bring us absolute delight with their vibrant colors and their uplifting songs, and the Bible's stories about birds help us feel as if we can glide alongside these carefree creatures. Imagine God's gentleness, soft as a feather, as you read: "Oh, that I had the wings of a dove! I would fly away and be at rest" (Ps. 55:6). Birds symbolize the freedom we find in loving God and following Jesus.

Read Genesis 1:20. Imagine God's joy as the first birds soared "across the vault of the sky." Let's flutter through a few other Bible stories about birds.

Atop Eagles' Wings

For Moses and the Israelites, Exodus 19:4 is a reminder of God's power to protect and rescue them: "You yourselves have seen what I did to Egypt, and how I carried you on eagles' wings and brought you to myself."

The imagery of eagles' wings was familiar to the Israelites. On their travels to the Promised Land it's likely that they watched a mother eagle flying with outstretched wings underneath her young as it learned to fly, ready to catch the fledgling and carry it back to the nest if necessary. Her wings often span six or seven feet, giving the young bird plenty of room to fall. God uses this beautiful and comforting image from nature to remind us that He protects us as gently and fiercely as a mother bird does her young.

Read what the Lord says in the next verse: "Now if you obey me fully and keep my covenant, then out of all nations you will be my treasured possession" (Ex. 19:5). Just as God claimed Israel His "treasured possession," He claims you and me today.

Because He claims us, God asks that we seek His wisdom as if it were a hidden treasure (Prov. 2:4). Where do we seek? In Colossians 2:3 Paul maps out our direct route: Jesus holds "all the treasures of wisdom and knowledge." Then in 2 Corinthians 4:7 Paul says, "We have this treasure in jars of clay to show that this all-surpassing power is from God and not from us." God places His love, wisdom, and knowledge inside us—"in jars of clay"—as a gift. God has a special plan and purpose for each one of us.

Scripture says that God claims us as His possessions, protects us like a mother eagle, and places His treasure inside us. Our goal is to find that treasure, declare it, and use our own unique, God-given talents and gifts to make the world a better place. Start today with your friends and family. What treasure inside yourself can you share with those closest to you?

Be an optimist. Demonstrate your faith. Use words that inspire and uplift. Help others feel they can soar like an eagle with the safety net of God's wings outstretched below them.

Forget Not

Read Psalm 103:1-5: "Praise the Lord, my soul; all my inmost being, praise his holy name. Praise the Lord, my soul, and forget not all his benefits—who forgives all your sins and heals all your diseases, who redeems your life from the pit and crowns you with love and compassion, who satisfies your desires with good things so that your youth is renewed like the eagle's."

Eagles are a symbol of power, strength, and victory. They can spend hours flying, gliding, looping, and even flying upside down. They can dive for prey at speeds of up to 150 miles per hour. Their keen eyesight allows them to spot prey up to one mile away. Like today, people in Bible times observe eagles living a long life, sometimes 30 years or more, which makes eagles an image of youth and vitality. Psalm 103 tells us, step by step, how to be grateful for the constant renewal we find in God, including "Forget not all his benefits" (verse 2).

What has God done for you?

Write down all the blessings from God you can think of, count them, and then take care not to forget His benefits.

God Cares

Read Psalm 104 for an eloquent account of how God cares for all of earth's creatures. Verses 27 and 28 say, "All creatures look to you to give them their food at the proper time. When you give it to them, they gather it up; when you open your hand, they are satisfied with good things." Likewise, Proverbs 23:5 reminds us to put our faith in God to provide for our needs and avoid getting attached to the things of this world. "Cast but a glance at riches, and they are gone, for they will surely sprout wings and fly off to the sky like an eagle."

First Kings 17 tells Elijah's prophecy of a great drought. But God promised Elijah that He would provide for his needs, telling him to live near a brook in the Kerith Ravine, east of the Jordan River, and drink from its waters. Elijah followed God's instructions and trusted Him to provide his daily food.

What sociable birds did Him send to bring food to Elijah each morning and each evening?

Thank God for providing for your needs today.

Doves of Peace

Read Genesis 8:6-12, the familiar story of Noah and the animals of the ark. At the end of the 40 days Noah opened the window and sent out a bird to scout the earth and the waters. What bird did he send out the first time?

The second bird Noah sent out was a dove. But the dove came back because waters still covered the earth. After waiting another seven days, Noah released the dove a second time. This time it returned with a fresh olive leaf in its beak, a symbol of peace between God and human beings, showing Noah that trees were starting to leaf out. Seven more days passed. When Noah released the dove for the third time, it did not return. The waters were receding from the earth, and Noah knew God was leading him toward a fresh start.

Read Matthew 3:13-17. After John baptized Jesus in the Jordan River, the Holy Spirit descended from heaven to show God's love for His Son. The Holy Spirit appeared as a bird. Which one?

God Knows the Number

Jesus assures us of our worth to God in Matthew 10:29-31. "Are not two sparrows sold for a penny? Yet not one of them will fall to the ground outside your Father's care. And even the very hairs of your head are all numbered. So don't be afraid; you are worth more than many sparrows."

Have you ever wondered how many hairs God actually counts on your head? In *Amazing Numbers in Biology* Rainer Flindt estimates that redheads such as the "ruddy" King David (1 Sam. 16:12, KJV) have about 90,000. Those with hair like King Solomon's, "black as a raven" (S. of Sol. 5:11), have about 100,000 hairs on their heads. Brown-haired people have 110,000 hairs, and people with blond hair 150,000.

Regardless of the color and number of hairs on our heads, Jesus uses the image of the small, fluttering sparrow to deliver the message of God's huge love for us. Christian speaker Norman Vincent Peale gave this advice: "Every day of your life [think] of yourself as living in partnership and companionship with Jesus Christ. If He actually walked by your side, would you be worried or afraid? Well, then, say to yourself, 'He is with me' " (*The Power of Positive Thinking*).

Vision of Home

Psalm 84:1-5 uses the image of birds as a guide for our journey home to God. It starts out in verses 1 and 2 by declaring how lovely God's dwelling place is and then conveying one's utmost desire to be united with God in heaven. It then continues: "Even the sparrow has found a home, and the swallow a nest for herself, where she may have her young—a place near your altar, Lord Almighty, my King and my God. Blessed are those who dwell in your house; they are ever praising you. Blessed are those whose strength is in you, whose hearts are set on pilgrimage."

Prayer Focus

Dear God, thank You for the pleasure birds bring to us with their dazzling colors and jubilant songs. Watching a bird soar the skies carries our thoughts toward heaven and toward You, dear Lord. In a bird's ability to fly we imagine our ability to do all things with Your help. Amen.

Zoom Lens

When Jesus told His disciples to go into the world to do His work, He told them to be as innocent as this bird. Find the answer in Matthew 10:16. Watching this bird's flight also brings gentleness and peace to mind. For Christians, this bird is a sign of baptism, the Holy Spirit, faithfulness, Jesus' victory, and forgiveness.

Action Shot

Grab your binoculars and go bird-watching today. Take along your Bible and read Isaiah 60:1: "Arise, shine, for your light has come, and the glory of the Lord rises upon you"; and Isaiah 60:8: "Who are these that fly along like clouds, like doves to their nests?" Listen to the birds sing, then read Song of Songs 2:12: "Flowers appear on the earth; the season of singing has come, the cooing of doves is heard in our land."

Birds sing for many different reasons; to communicate with other birds and to protect their territory are two of them. But their lilting songs seem to exhibit the art of rising up in gratitude.

Today, rise up. Be happy simply because you are God's child.

Chapter 10

Beasts: Teachers and Best Friends

As the deer pants for streams of water,
so my soul pants for you, my God.
—Psalm 42:1

Animals are such agreeable friends," wrote nineteenth-century English novelist George Eliot. "They ask no questions, they pass no criticisms."

By giving us animals as a gift, God created amazing teachers and helpmates. The animals of the Bible carry us, coach us, protect us, share with us, befriend us, and make us smile. In many of the Bible's most dramatic stories animals play vital roles, and the Scriptures often refer to animals with gratitude and tenderness.

Animal stories contain symbols of God's promises. In Genesis 6:19 God instructed Noah to "bring into the ark two of all living creatures, male and female, to keep them alive with you."

Job reminded his friends that God is in control, even in times of anguish: "But ask the animals, and they will teach you, or the birds in the sky, and they will tell you; or speak to the earth, and it will teach you, or let the fish in the sea inform you. Which of all these does not know that the hand of the Lord has done this? In his hand is the life of every creature and the breath of all mankind" (Job 12:7-10).

Imagine the manger scene at Jesus' birth, with Mary and Joseph surrounded by their animal companions.

Read 1 Samuel 9. What lost animals does Saul seek when he runs into the prophet Samuel, who will proclaim Saul king? Let's trek through the Old and New Testaments in our quest for other stories about animals.

A Shepherd's Job

Adam and Eve's son Abel is the first of many shepherds we encounter in the Bible (Gen. 4). A shepherd's job is to lead the flock to green pastures and springs of fresh water. Shepherds also protect their sheep from danger. Now go to Genesis 29:9 to discover the name of Jacob's future wife, who was a shepherd tending her father's sheep.

David was a young boy shepherding his father's sheep when the prophet Samuel sent for him (1 Sam. 16). Later David explained to King Saul that although he was small in stature, he was well able to defeat the giant Goliath because he often protected his father's sheep from lions and bears (1 Sam. 17). David knew that God was with him and trusted God's power to keep him safe.

David later wrote the famous line "The Lord is my shepherd" to begin Psalm 23, known as the shepherd psalm.

Calling the Sheep by Name

Since tending sheep was a natural pastime for many people in Bible times, Jesus often used the familiar image of sheep to teach His followers. In John 10:1-5 Jesus began with a warning to the Pharisees, saying, "Anyone who does not enter the sheep pen by the gate, but climbs in by some other way, is a thief and a robber." He then continued by drawing a comparison: "The one who enters by the gate is the shepherd of the sheep. . . . The sheep listen to his voice. He calls his own sheep by name and leads them out. When he has brought out all his own, he goes on ahead of them, and his sheep follow him because they know his voice. But they will never follow a stranger; in fact, they will run away from him because they do not recognize a stranger's voice."

Do you believe you are able to hear God's voice? Jesus says our answer should be a resounding "Yes!"

When Jesus calls and you answer, you belong to Him. You are one of God's own. Jesus says that God opens the gate as He calls, and we are to follow Him through the gateway. Jesus referred to His divinity in this verse: "The one who enters by the gate is the shepherd."

The shepherd—the leader, protector, and guide of the flock—calls their sheep by name. Jesus knows your name and mine. Having a relationship with God, with Jesus, is like having a relationship with a very best friend. Spend time talking to God and praying, and then spend time listening for God's answer. Tell God your concerns and your joys, and listen for His answers.

God's answer may come in a voice you hear in your mind, often called the conscience, our built-in sense of right and wrong. His answer may come through a Bible text or even in the voice of a friend. Or God's answer may simply be a feeling of peace in your heart. Practice listening to God, and you'll get better and better at hearing Him.

The Sheep Gate

Ten gates connected the protective wall around ancient Jerusalem that was destroyed during the Babylonian invasion around 586 B.C. The book of Nehemiah tells how Nehemiah, a wine taster for the king of Persia, got permission to lead a group of men to Jerusalem to rebuild the broken wall around the city.

Read Nehemiah 3, a detailed account of how Nehemiah and his men rebuilt and restored the wall. Nehemiah begins with the Sheep Gate in Nehemiah 3:1: "Eliashib the high priest and his fellow priests went to work and rebuilt the Sheep Gate. They dedicated it and set its doors in place, building as far as the Tower of the Hundred, which they dedicated, and as far as the Tower of Hananel."

Travel with Nehemiah and his men, counterclockwise, around the full length of the wall of Jerusalem in Nehemiah 3. The last verse takes us full circle, ending where it began, at the Sheep Gate: "And between the room above the corner and the Sheep Gate the goldsmiths and merchants made repairs" (verse 32).

John 5:2 tells us that in New Testament times the Sheep Gate was near the healing pools of Bethesda. "Now there is in Jerusalem near the Sheep Gate a pool, which in Aramaic is called Bethesda and which is surrounded by five covered colonnades." John tells us this is the site of one of Jesus' healing miracles. (See chapter 14 for a detailed account.)

In the Old Testament the Sheep Gate, near the Temple, was opened as sheep were led in for sacrifice. While we no longer sacrifice animals as part of worship, the Sheep Gate symbolizes the importance of worship. In the New Testament the image of a sheep gate takes on new meaning.

Read Jesus' words in John 10:7-10: "Very truly I tell you, I am the gate for the sheep. All who have come before me are thieves and robbers, but the sheep have not listened to them. I am the gate; whoever enters through me will be saved. They will come in and go out, and find pasture. The thief comes only to steal and kill and destroy; I have come that they may have life, and have it to the full."

Jesus is our gateway, our entryway, our solid, firm pathway. He leads us to a relationship with the Divine. Jesus leads us on a narrow pathway with solid, firm footing. If our foot slips from the path, the Good Shepherd is there to reach out His hand. He will catch us and pull us back onto the path. Jesus is not only the gateway; He is the way to living abundantly, to have life "to the full." Life abundant, through Jesus, is a life filled with grace, joy, peace, and prosperity. Jesus' wish is that you claim your abundant life in Him today.

One Flock, One Shepherd

Jesus uses the words "I am the good shepherd" twice. In John 10:11 Jesus says, "I am the good shepherd. The good shepherd lays down his life for the sheep." In John 10:14-16 Jesus repeats, "I am the good shepherd; I know my sheep and my sheep know me—just as the Father knows me and I know the Father—and I lay down my life for the sheep. I have other sheep that are not of this sheep pen. I must bring them also. They too will listen to my voice, and there shall be one flock and one shepherd."

Jesus is saying, once and for all, that He calls each one of us. "I have other sheep that are not of this sheep pen. I must bring them also." The Good Shepherd's other names are High Priest, Redeemer, and Deliverer. Jesus calls each of us by name. Jesus shepherds us home.

A Man Healed on Sabbath

One Sabbath Jesus visited a synagogue where He noticed "a man with a shriveled hand." The Pharisees asked Him, "Is it lawful to heal on the Sabbath?" Jesus answered, "If any of you has a sheep and it falls into a pit on the Sabbath, will you not take hold of it and lift it out? How much more valuable is a person than a sheep! Therefore it is lawful to do good on the Sabbath." Then Jesus said to the man, "Stretch out your hand." The man extended his hand to Jesus, and it was completely healed (Matt. 12:9-13).

Genesis 2:2 tells us that "by the seventh day God had finished the work he had been doing; so on the seventh day he rested from all his work." God intends the Sabbath to be a day of rest from our duties. But Jesus elaborates. If you see an opportunity to do a good work or to help another, do so, any day and any time, even on the Sabbath.

Read John 21:15-17. How many times does Jesus ask Peter if he loves Him before issuing the command "Feed my sheep"?

Today many churches call their leader "pastor." The word *pastor* comes from the Latin verb *pascere*, which means "to feed." Pastors feed their congregations spiritually by following Jesus' example.

The Wolf and the Lamb

Isaiah is the book to go through to find Old Testament insights about the first time Jesus came to this earth. Isaiah 11:1-9 is one such passage. It starts out with an image that hearkens back to our exploration of various plants in Section One: "A shoot will come up from the stump of Jesse [King David's father]; from his roots a Branch will bear fruit" (verse 1). Similarly, in 2 Samuel 7:11-16 God promises that a descendant of David (from the stump of Jesse) will arrive as the Messiah who rules forever. Jesus confirms this prophecy in John 15:1-4 when He calls Himself a grapevine and God His gardener. Jesus asks us to remain in Him, in the vine, and we are the fruit He bears.

Isaiah 11:2-5 gives us important attributes about this Branch, the coming Messiah—Jesus: "The Spirit of the Lord will rest on him. . . . With righteousness he will judge the needy, with justice he will give decisions for the poor of the earth. He will strike the earth with the rod of his mouth; with the breath of his lips he will slay the wicked. Righteousness will be his belt and faithfulness the sash around his waist."

And now, if you continue reading our passage in Isaiah 11, you will discover that the Bible also uses animals to illustrate more truth about Jesus: "The wolf will live with the lamb, the leopard will lie down with the goat, the calf and the lion and the yearling together; and a little child will lead them. The cow will feed with the bear, their young will lie down together, and the lion will eat straw like the ox. . . . They will neither harm nor destroy on all my holy mountain, for the earth will be full of the knowledge of the Lord as the waters cover the sea" (verses 6-9). By using the image of animals at peace with one another, Isaiah provides a glimpse of the goodwill the Prince of Peace (Isa. 9:6) will bring on earth. Psalm 37:11 foreshadows the peace Jesus teaches in the Sermon on the Mount: "The meek will inherit the land and enjoy peace and prosperity." Jesus claimed the peacemakers are the children of God (Matt. 5:9).

Out of the Lion's Mouth: The Decrees of King Darius

Daniel 6 tells the familiar story of Daniel and the lions. Daniel, a Jewish teenager, was exiled to Babylon after Jerusalem's downfall. As the years went by, he distinguished himself as a trusted administrator for King Darius. However, the king's administrators were jealous of Daniel and looked for a way to discredit him. They convinced the king to pass a "decree that anyone who prays to any god or human being during the next thirty days, except to you, Your Majesty, shall be thrown into the lions' den" (verse 7).

"Now when Daniel learned that the decree had been published, he went home to his upstairs room where the windows opened toward Jerusalem. Three times a day he got down on his knees and prayed, giving thanks to his God, just as he had done before" (verse 10).

The men who convinced King Darius to make this decree made sure that he followed through on the punishment. The king was distraught because he knew Daniel was a good man and he realized he had been tricked. But he had no choice but to have Daniel thrown into the lions' den!

Before this happened, the king said to Daniel, "May your God, whom you serve continually, rescue you" (verse 16).

The next morning King Darius rushed to the lions' den and called loudly to Daniel. Daniel answered back that his God had shut the lions' mouths and that he was unhurt.

King Darius was overjoyed and immediately made "a decree that in every part of my kingdom people must fear and reverence the God of Daniel. 'For he is the living God and he endures forever'" (verse 26).

Lost and Found

Jesus' parables show His followers God's love and devotion to them. Let's look at the parable of the lost sheep in Luke 15:1-7. In this passage we see people who were generally shunned gathering around Jesus. Upon seeing Jesus' receptiveness to them, "the Pharisees and the teachers of the law muttered, 'This man welcomes sinners and eats with them.'" Jesus' response was gentle to both the outcasts and the Pharisees who looked down upon them: "Suppose one of you has a hundred sheep and loses one of them. Doesn't he leave the ninety-nine in the open country and go after the lost sheep until he finds it? And when he finds it, he joyfully puts it on his shoulders and goes home. Then he calls his friends and neighbors together and says, 'Rejoice with me; I have found my lost sheep.'" Jesus paints a picture of His love for us, His sheep. And as if this divine expression of love weren't enough, He adds, "I tell you that in the same way there will be more rejoicing in heaven over one sinner who repents than over ninety-nine righteous persons who do not need to repent." Jesus uses the familiar image of a lost sheep in the field to express God's never-ending desire to bring us home to a relationship with Him.

A Prodigal and Pigs

Luke 15:11-32 contains Jesus' parable of the lost son. Notice how Jesus uses pigs, which are intelligent animals, to bring the prodigal son to his senses. The lost son is so hungry that he wants to eat the pods (possibly carob pods) that he sees the pigs eat. The father in this parable welcomes home the son who was lost but also reassures the older son, who never left, that he is equally loved.

Which son are you most similar to? Whether you are new to Jesus' teachings or have strayed from your faith in God, celebrate the welcome Jesus says will be prepared for your homecoming. If you've been a faithful follower all or most of your life, you may feel like the older son. He stands beside his father saying, "I remained beside you all these years! I've been faithful! Why aren't you throwing a party for me?" Hear God's reassurance gleaned from Jesus' parable: "I'm grateful that you are always with me, and everything I have is yours. Nothing is taken away from you to celebrate with your brother. My love and goodness is abundant; there is plenty for everyone. I love each one of you equally!"

The Hardworking Donkey

Read Jesus' parable of the good Samaritan in Luke 10:25-37. In this story Jesus has a deep conversation with a law expert who wants to earn eternal life. The lawyer quotes the law, "Love your neighbor as yourself," but wants clarification. "Who is my neighbor?" he asks. With the parable of the good Samaritan, Jesus answers, Everyone.

Going a step further, Jesus answers the unasked question *How* do I love others? When the Samaritan saw the injured man, perhaps he asked himself, *Why* should I show love to this man? When we look at someone else, Jesus would want us to remember that He loves that person, and He wants *us* to treat them with love too.

When the Samaritan put the injured man on his own donkey, he was following the Golden Rule Jesus outlined in Luke 6:31: "Do to others as you would have them do to you."

The gentle, indispensible donkey carried out a great service by carrying the man to the inn. Donkeys are hardworking animals valued for their stamina and protective instincts. Modern farmers often place a single donkey in a field of cattle or horses. Donkeys have excellent "radar" and protect the herd from potential threats such as snakes and coyotes. The donkey in this story likely protected the injured man on their journey to the inn.

What is the name of the One you will call on when you need protection?

Riding Like a King

When Joseph and Mary traveled to Bethlehem for the census, it is likely that Mary, pregnant with Baby Jesus, rode a donkey, for that was a common mode of transportation in Bible times (Luke 2:1-7).

Jesus was born in Bethlehem, near Jerusalem, but grew up in Nazareth, in the northern part of Galilee. He spent most of His adult life in the communities surrounding the Sea of Galilee. Near the end of His life Jesus came full circle. He traveled back toward Jerusalem to celebrate the Festival of the Passover and stayed with His friends Lazarus, Mary, and Martha in nearby Bethany.

At a dinner to honor Jesus, Martha served, and her sister Mary came in and anointed the feet of Jesus with expensive nard (John 12:1-3). The next morning Jesus and His disciples traveled into Jerusalem.

There the people who had come out to see Him waved palm branches, a sign of victory, as they waited for their King's arrival. Some people shouted, "Hosanna," a Hebrew word that means "save" or "help." They sang the psalm of old, "Blessed is he who comes in the name of the Lord!" (Ps. 118:26). Some people may have expected their King to ride a magnificent horse in victory, but prophecy had foretold something different. John 12:12-15 tells us that Jesus arrived in Jerusalem, fulfilling Scripture by riding a young donkey.

"Rejoice greatly, Daughter Zion! Shout, Daughter Jerusalem! See, your king comes to you, righteous and victorious, lowly and riding on a donkey, on a colt, the foal of a donkey" (Zech. 9:9). Donkeys are an amazing combination of features—hardworking and strong, yet gentle and patient. Perhaps this is why Jesus chose this humble creature to carry Him home.

Prayer Focus

Dear God, thank You for the gift of animals and the happiness they bring to our lives. Some animals are best friends, and some are simply a joy to behold. Help us to honor animals as part of Your creation and always remember that all living creatures are precious to You. Amen.

Zoom Lens

Read Mark 5:1-17. How many animals did Jesus include in this miraculous healing?

Few of us are as troubled as the demon-possessed man was, but we all have troubling thoughts from time to time. Whenever you are hurt or upset, pray to Jesus. He can help take those troubles away.

Action Shot

Job 39 contains one of the most beautiful poems in the Bible. Read God's talk with Job about the beauty of animals. Find a quiet moment and write your own poem about animals today. Choose any style of poem that you wish—rhyming, free verse, acrostic, haiku, or other. Ask a friend to join you in the endeavor.

Chapter 11

Bugs: Weaving Life's Plan

Ants are creatures of little strength, yet they store up their food in the summer.
—Proverbs 30:25

Unless you live on the North or South Pole, you live with bugs. Bugs creep and crawl across deserts and forests. They live in the grass at your feet and the trees overhead. Bugs climb mountaintops and burrow underground. Dragonflies fly, butterflies glide, flies do somersaults, crickets chirp, moths build cocoons, grasshoppers jump 50 times their length, bees make honey, and fireflies light up their abdomens. Ladybugs and praying mantises are "good" bugs because they eat other bugs, and that helps keep earth's plants healthy. Whether you think bugs are interesting or icky, they fulfill the role God has given them. We too can find our place in God's plan.

Read Luke 11:11-13. In verse 12 Jesus uses the frightening scorpion to bring home the point that God willingly helps those who ask Him. Let's look at other Bible stories that use earth's tiny bugs to illustrate God's power to sustain His children and thus teach life lessons.

Would You Eat Bugs?

To convince the Egyptian pharaoh to let God's people go, one of the ways God showed His power was by sending a swarm of locusts that devoured every green thing in the fields (Ex. 10:1-13). And even today, locusts cause considerable damage to crops in the Holy Land. There are more than 50 known species of locusts in Palestine; they fly over crops in swarms that resemble dark clouds. One "mob" can cover up to 2,000 square miles and eat everything green that grows.

The book of Proverbs describes locusts as "little and wise," saying, "locusts have no king, yet they advance together in ranks" (Prov. 30:27).

Locusts are mentioned again in Leviticus 11:21, 22 as God tells Moses and Aaron which insects they may eat: "There are, however, some flying insects that walk on all fours that you may eat: those that have jointed legs for hopping on the ground. Of these you may eat any kind of locust, katydid, cricket or grasshopper." Locusts were still used as food in New Testament times, for we read that John the Baptist ate locusts with wild honey (Mark 1:6). Today some residents of the Holy Land and other places still eat locusts for their protein.

A Spider's Web

Take a walk in the early morning before the dew has settled, and somewhere along the way you're likely to discover a spider's web. Spiders build their webs in every imaginable place—between trees and fence posts and on walls and windows. Some spiders spin silk from tiny body organs called spinnerets. Fast silk-spinners, spiders can build a complex web in just an hour or so. Spiders build many types of webs—tangled webs, sheet webs, funnel webs, triangle webs, and orb webs. They use the webs to catch insects for food.

Spiders fill an important role in nature by helping to control earth's insect population.

If you look at a spider's web from your own perspective, it appears fragile. If the web is in your way, all you need to do is move it aside with your finger or pick up a small stick and knock it down.

But imagine a spider's web from the viewpoint of a fly or other small insect. Flying or stumbling into the web is a deadly trap. The web appears huge and forbidding. The silk threads are so strong and sticky that there is no escape. And as soon as the spider feels the vibration caused by the fly or other insect, it rushes to its prey to make sure it doesn't get away.

Read Job 8:13-15. Job's friend Bildad uses the image of a spider's web to remind Job to put his faith in God. Bildad says if we put our faith in anything other than God, what we "trust in is fragile," what we "rely on is a spider's web." Perhaps Bildad is saying that when we put our faith in God, He will hold us up no matter what trials we face.

Throughout the book of Job, Job wrestles with the question of why bad things happen to good people, why good people pray and disasters still come.

Job 1:1 tells us that Job was "blameless," that he had done nothing to bring on his troubles. But despite that, all of Job's children were killed, his servants were killed, the buildings on Job's estate were destroyed, and, last, Job lost his health. Even his riches could not save him; Job lost that, too.

Have you ever wondered why bad things happen to good people?

And why do good things seem to happen to bad people?

The book of Job asks the same questions.

Job's trials include his three friends Eliphaz, Bildad, and Zophar.

These friends traveled a long way to be with him, and they surely had good intentions, but telling Job that his problems were his own fault surely added to his suffering.

Job argued with them, and he even argued with God. But eventually Job completely surrendered to God.

An Italian proverb says, "Begin your web and God will supply the thread." Perhaps Job realized that he and his friends were woven and bound together like the threads of a spider's web. Job showed love to his friends, and the Bible says, "After Job had prayed for his friends, the Lord restored his fortunes and gave him twice as much as he had before" (Job 42:10). Scripture says Job lived another 140 years, and the second half of Job's life was even more blessed than the first.

An author of a book said there are two types of people in the world—evaluators and affirmers. In this story Job's three friends fall into the evaluator category. They *evaluate* him. They criticize, judge, and point out all of Job's faults. It's painful to watch Job endure this, and it's even more excruciating when we experience it ourselves.

This author calls the other kind of people affirmers. These people *affirm* us. They call out our good points.

In her book *Balcony People* Joyce Landorf Heatherley suggests that another word for the affirmers is "balcony people," for they stand in the balcony of our lives and cheer us on. They speak words of encouragement. They treat us with honor and respect. They are always on our side. They root for us.

Job is a good example of God's command to love all people. Job loved his friends even when they were difficult to love. Most important, Job prayed for them. When we encounter evaluators in life, we can pray for them and ask God to help us find the qualities that are lovable and praiseworthy in them. But we can also surround ourselves with balcony people, people who genuinely see our good qualities and lift us up by affirming our positive traits.

Treasures in Heaven

We think of spiders as insects, but they actually belong to the arachnid family. Spiders differ from insects in that spiders have eight legs, two body parts, and no antennae. Insects, in contrast, have six legs, three main body parts, and two antennae.

Eighteenth-century English poet Alexander Pope wrote in his *Essay on Man*, "The spider's touch, how exquisitely fine! Feels at each thread, and lives along the line."

Spiders are well known for their silken webs, but one insect, the silkworm moth, produces a silk cocoon.

There are more than 200 species of moths and butterflies *(Lepidoptera)* in the Holy Land. Butterflies are active during the day, while moths fly at night. Jesus used the image of a moth's ability to destroy things to teach His followers that material things don't matter. Loving God is our most valuable possession. "Do not store up for yourselves treasures on earth, where moths and vermin destroy, and where thieves break in and steal. But store up for yourselves treasures in heaven, where moths and vermin do not destroy, and where thieves do not break in and steal. For where your treasure is, there your heart will be also" (Matt. 6:19-21).

A Bug's Design

Two of earth's insects symbolize Christ in the manner that God designed them. If you spot a green or brown praying mantis camouflaged among nearby grass or leaves, observe it for a few moments. Notice the bulging eyes on its triangular head. When it searches for prey, the praying mantis can swivel its head by 180 degrees. Gardeners consider the mantis a beneficial insect because it catches and eats other insects with its lightning-fast reflexes. With its front legs angularly bent in an apparent attitude of prayer, the praying mantis is a fascinating, visual reminder to pray.

The colorful butterflies you see drinking nectar from flowers are in the fourth stage of their life. The butterfly's metamorphosis, or change, begins with an egg that grows into a caterpillar that turns into a chrysalis that finally emerges as a butterfly. Imagine a butterfly's sense of freedom as it breaks free of its chrysalis. Think of Jesus after His long night in the Garden of Gethsemane, His trial, and His crucifixion. Imagine the freedom He surely felt when resurrected from the tomb. Jesus promises to share His rebirth, His new life, with us. Following Jesus helps us feel as free as a butterfly.

Prayer Focus

Dear God, we find it easy to admire a regal butterfly floating on the wind as a living symbol of Jesus' resurrection. When we look at other creeping, crawling creatures, some of us don't find them as easy to love. It can be the same with people, dear Lord. Some are easy for us to love and some are not. Help us to remember today that all living things and all people are under Your control and protection, and that You ask us to show love and respect to all living things. We thank You for Your love and protection for each of us. Amen.

Zoom Lens

If you've ever gone on a picnic, you've likely been visited by ants. A colony of ants works as a team and constantly scouts for food. When one ant finds a treat, it rushes to tell the others. Have you noticed that ants often march in a straight line toward the food? They are following the scent trail left by another ant to give a precise roadmap to the food.

Read Proverbs 6:6-8. Whatever task is set before you today, work as hard as an ant and help others by being a team player.

Action Shot

Grab a shovel and find a small plot of earth where you can dig. Does the dirt have holes in it? Perhaps an earthworm recently tunneled through, creating air pockets underground to help grass, plants, flowers, and trees grow. All living creatures, including bugs, serve a purpose on earth. Read Colossians 3:1-17 and spend today living verse 17: "Whatever you do, whether in word or deed, do it all in the name of the Lord Jesus, giving thanks to God the Father through him."

Section Four

Biblical Elements of Truth: Earth, Air, Water, and Fire

Praise the Lord, my soul.
Lord my God, you are very great;
you are clothed with splendor and majesty.
The Lord wraps himself in light as with a garment;
he stretches out the heavens like a tent
and lays the beams of his upper chambers on their waters.
He makes the clouds his chariot
and rides on the wings of the wind.
He makes winds his messengers,
flames of fire his servants.
He set the earth on its foundations;
it can never be moved.
You covered it with the watery depths as with a garment.
—Psalm 104:1-6

Chapter 12

Earth: A Solid Foundation

The earth is filled with your love, Lord; teach me your decrees.
—Psalm 119:64

Sit beside Jesus on the hillside, on the Mount of Beatitudes near Capernaum. Feel the breeze blow in from the nearby Sea of Galilee. Hear the leaves rustle on the olive trees. Wiggle your toes in the grass. Rest your hands on the soft earth and listen to the voice of Jesus speaking the Beatitudes (Matt. 5:3-5), the opening words of His Sermon on the Mount. Jesus utters a series of statements beginning with "Blessed are . . ."; He declares that the blessed ones are "the poor in spirit," "those who mourn," "the meek," "those who hunger and thirst for righteousness," "the merciful," "the pure in heart," "the peacemakers," and "those who are persecuted." To these people Jesus promises eternal, heavenly blessings and rewards.

Read Amos 4:13. Who does this say treads on the heights of the earth?

From Old Testament to New, let's traverse a wide landscape in search of the Bible's earth stories.

Holy Ground

"God called the dry ground 'land,' . . . and saw that it was good" (Gen. 1:10). The rich, brown earth is solid, stable, and able to bear a load. Earth drinks in the sunlight and provides nutritious soil to help green things grow. The earth encompasses valleys, mountains, gardens, hilltops, and bodies of water. Earth hides treasures of minerals, jewels, and rocks within it. Read 1 Samuel 17:40. How many smooth stones did David scoop from earth's stream before he went to face the giant Goliath? In what secret place did David later hide from Saul (1 Sam. 24:1-4)?

When God appeared to Moses in a burning bush, He said, "Do not come any closer. . . . Take off your sandals, for the place where you are standing is holy ground"

(Ex. 3:5). Isaiah 6:3 proclaims, "Holy, holy, holy is the Lord Almighty; the whole earth is full of his glory."

A Stone Pillow

Read Genesis 28:10-22. Jacob was following orders from his father, Isaac, to travel to Paddan Aram, or northwest Mesopotamia, to find a wife. Jacob stopped for the night and chose one of earth's smooth stones for a pillow. His dreams that night showed him an angel's staircase leading from earth to heaven. God spoke to Jacob in his dream: "I am the Lord, the God of your father Abraham and the God of Isaac. I will give you and your descendants the land on which you are lying. . . . All peoples on earth will be blessed through you and your offspring. I am with you and will watch over you wherever you go, and I will bring you back to this land. I will not leave you until I have done what I have promised you."

Jacob awoke from his dream in a state of awe. He believed that plot of earth to be the house of God, the gateway to heaven. Jacob turned his stone pillow upright like a pillar and poured oil on it. He called the land Bethel, which means "house of God," and pledged his faithfulness to God.

Spending time outdoors as Jacob did is a powerful way to invite God's presence in your life. Is there a spot on earth where you feel especially close to God? Find a favorite stone to sit on, or lie down the way Jacob did. Pray what is on your heart or simply listen to God.

The Still Small Voice on the Mountaintop

Read 1 Kings 19:1-13. Elijah traveled 40 days and 40 nights to reach Mount Horeb, the mountain of God sometimes called Mount Sinai, on which Moses first saw God in a burning bush (Ex. 3:1-3) and later received the Ten Commandments (Ex. 20).

There on the mountaintop God spoke to Elijah; He said, "Go out and stand on the mountain in the presence of the Lord, for the Lord is about to pass by" (1 Kings 19:11). What followed was a series of dramatic and literally earth-shattering forces of nature—a wind, earthquake, and fire. The passage tells us that in each of those natural elements, the Lord was in fact "not in" them. However, "after the fire came a gentle whisper. When Elijah heard it, he pulled his cloak over his face and went out and stood at the mouth of the cave. Then a voice said to him, 'What are you doing here, Elijah?'" (verses 12, 13).

God used the wind, the earthquake, and the fire to get Elijah's attention. And then, when Elijah was ready to listen, God spoke in the form of that still small voice. When was the last time you sat and simply listened for God's voice inside of you? The still small voice Elijah heard is what you and I call our conscience. God's voice tells us right from wrong. God's voice leads us on the right path.

Life in our modern world seems to move so fast that many times we don't hear this still small voice. Even the lives of children and teens may be packed full of activities. There is school, homework, and, for some of you, a job, and then there's all the time we spend watching TV, playing video games, listening to the iPod—and more. It's hard to hear God's voice with all that noise in our ears.

Today is the day to slow down. If possible, go outside and take a walk on a wooded path. Climb a hill. Sit in a field. Take a moment to listen intently as Elijah did. Ground yourself. Clear your mind of all the chatter of daily life and simply listen for the still small voice of God. It's perfectly OK if you don't hear an audible sound as Elijah did. Sometimes the still small voice of God simply *feels* like peace.

Read John 11:17-37. Notice how intently Jesus listened to Martha and Mary. He listened with more than His ears; He listened with His heart. His compassion for them was so strong that "Jesus wept" (John 11:35).

When was the last time you sat and truly listened to what a friend said? How often do you brush off your brother or sister when they want to talk to you? When was the last time you sat down and really talked—and listened—to your grandma or grandpa? When was the last time you felt someone truly listened to you?

In *Desiderata,* poet Max Ehrmann writes, "Speak your truth quietly and clearly; and listen to others."

Practice the art of listening today.

Salt of the Earth

Jesus told His followers, "You are the salt of the earth. But if the salt loses its saltiness, how can it be made salty again? It is no longer good for anything, except to be thrown out and trampled underfoot" (Matt. 5:13).

The people listening to Jesus were familiar with the salt clusters, or pillars, that form in the waters of the Dead Sea. The 156-mile-long Jordan River flows south. Dropping first into the Sea of Galilee, the river continues meandering southward until it ends at the Dead Sea. The lowest place on earth, the Dead Sea is 1,300 feet below sea level. As the Jordan River nears the Dead Sea, the water becomes saltier and saltier. The water has no place to escape from the Dead Sea. Instead, it evaporates and leaves salt behind. With a saline content of 22 to 30 percent, nothing can live in the Dead Sea. Shallow waters in the Dead Sea are so thick with salt that the water looks like ice. Salt from the Dead Sea covers the surrounding cliffs, and the earth near the Dead Sea is too salty for farming. Salt, which was often mined from the Dead Sea, was a valuable preservative in Bible times and was used to dry and preserve fish and other foods.

In modern times we often ask if a person is "worth their salt." Jesus assures us in

Matthew 5 that we are! Using salt as a symbol of worthiness, Jesus says every person is valuable to God. By encouraging His followers to maintain their saltiness, Jesus inspires us to be strong and pure in our faith. He tells us to continue seeking wisdom and knowledge by studying His teachings. The apostle Paul uses salt as an image of friendship, advising, "Let your conversation be always full of grace, seasoned with salt, so that you may know how to answer everyone" (Col. 4:6).

Zion's Stone

Read the parable of the Wise and Foolish Builders in Matthew 7:24-29: "Therefore everyone who hears these words of mine and puts them into practice is like a wise man who built his house on the rock. The rain came down, the streams rose, and the winds blew and beat against that house; yet it did not fall, because it had its foundation on the rock. But everyone who hears these words of mine and does not put them into practice is like a foolish man who built his house on sand. The rain came down, the streams rose, and the winds blew and beat against that house, and it fell with a great crash."

A firm foundation is necessary for building projects. In construction, builders sometimes begin with a cornerstone, a foundation upon which they line up the other stones. Isaiah explains God's plan for a firm foundation for His people: "So this is what the Sovereign Lord says: 'See, I lay a stone in Zion, a tested stone, a precious cornerstone for a sure foundation; the one who relies on it will never be stricken with panic'" (Isa. 28:16). The apostle Peter echoes Isaiah's prophecy to new believers in 1 Peter 2:6.

Have you ever climbed atop a tall boulder in a park or along a hiking trail? Some boulders weigh tons. They are immovable. Jesus calls Himself the Rock we build our faith on. He is permanent, stable, and reliable. Jesus says that to build our house on rock, we must hear and follow His teachings. Read John 20:1. Build your house on the rock that moved the stone that should have been immovable.

Earth Treasures

Listen to Jesus teach the parables of the hidden treasure and the pearl: "The kingdom of heaven is like treasure hidden in a field. When a man found it, he hid it again, and then in his joy went and sold all he had and bought that field. Again, the kingdom of heaven is like a merchant looking for fine pearls. When he found one of great value, he went away and sold everything he had and bought it." In these two parables Jesus seeks to ignite our passion for following God. He tells us that a person who finds the pathway to God will stop at nothing to follow it. Jesus is our treasure map. He knows the way home. All we have to do is follow Him (Matt. 13:44, 45).

Prayer Focus

Dear God, thank You for the precious earth, the home You've given us while we learn the life lessons You plan for us. Help us to treat the earth and all its inhabitants with loving, reverent care. Amen.

Zoom Lens

Read Luke 4:1-13. Jesus spent 40 days wandering along the rugged valleys and barren summits in the dry, desert wilderness of Judea, the southern part of the Holy Land. How many times was Jesus tempted to stray from God? Jesus used Scripture to turn back each temptation.

Then when Jesus faced His greatest trial, He sought refuge in a beautiful, open-air sanctuary, the Garden of Gethsemane (Matt. 26:36-56). How many times did Jesus pray in the garden? What is your favorite scripture or prayer, one that brings you back to the peace of God when you need it most?

Action Shot

"Go out in joy and be led forth in peace; the mountains and hills will burst into song before you, and all the trees of the field will clap their hands" (Isa. 55:12). Find a favorite spot on the earth—atop freshly mown grass, under a shade tree, in a field of flowers, or beside a flowing stream. Watch the sunlight sparkle, creating prisms of light around you. Read Malachi 3:16-18 (KJV). Thank God for claiming you as one of His jewels, for writing your name in His book of remembrance. Look for the jewel-like light in God's other children today.

Chapter 13

Air:
Faith Invisible

The wind blows wherever it pleases. You hear its sound, but you cannot tell where it comes from or where it is going. So it is with everyone born of the Spirit.
—John 3:8

"The best and most beautiful things in the world cannot be seen or even touched—they must be felt with the heart," Helen Keller once wrote. Air, the invisible element, is as real as God's love. At times air is still. When it moves, we feel air as wind, sometimes blistering and sometimes blustery. Air is subtle, incorporeal, ethereal, and fleeting, yet it can be forceful and potent.

Though invisible, breath *is* life, as Genesis 2:7 says: "The Lord God formed a man from the dust of the ground and breathed into his nostrils the breath of life, and the man became a living being."

The cycle of breath, inhaling and exhaling, symbolizes the rhythm and flow of life and death. We see our breath only on cold days; we see the wind only when air stirs what lies in its path. The wind aids the growth of earth's green things by carrying pollen from flowering plant to flowering plant.

Isaiah 42:5, 6 tells us the source of breath, the giver of life: "This is what God the Lord says—the Creator of the heavens, who stretches them out, who spreads out the earth with all that springs from it, who gives breath to its people, and life to those who walk on it: 'I, the Lord, have called you in righteousness; I will take hold of your hand.' " The Holy Spirit and the breath symbolize each other. The Holy Spirit is often depicted as a dove hovering on the wind; wind is often portrayed as wings.

Read Job 38. Who speaks to Job out of a whirlwind? Who asks Job the questions that demonstrate the wise choice is always "Trust God," no matter what situation we face in life?

Let's explore other stories of biblical winds and discover the peace and tranquillity God offers us each day, even in the midst of life's storms.

A Whirlwind Where Two Were Gathered

Psalm 104:3, 4 says, "The Lord . . . rides on the wings of the wind. He makes winds his messengers." Read 2 Kings 2:1-11, a story with a message in the wind. Walk alongside Elijah and Elisha as they travel from Gilgal. Three times Elijah asked Elisha to stay behind, and three times Elisha refused his mentor, saying, "As surely as the Lord lives and as you live, I will not leave you." Elijah and Elisha traveled from Gilgal to Bethel to Jericho and finally to the Jordan River.

Elijah parted the waters of the Jordan with his cloak, and the pair crossed on dry ground between the waters. Elijah asked Elisha to make a request before they are parted, and Elisha said, "Let me inherit a double portion of your spirit" (verse 9). Elijah told Elisha that if he saw Elijah being taken to heaven with his own eyes, then his request would be granted. Verse 11 says, "As they were walking along and talking together, suddenly a chariot of fire and horses of fire appeared and separated the two of them, and Elijah went up to heaven in a whirlwind." Elisha saw Elijah depart and thus inherited a double portion of Elijah's spirit.

Jesus says that if two or more are gathered in His name, He is there also (Matt. 18:20), and Luke 10:1 says that Jesus sent His disciples out "two by two." God forms formidable partnerships among His people, like the partnership between Elijah and Elisha.

Think of a special friend you can thank God for today. God places special people in our lives to encourage us on our journey, but He reminds us that the most prevailing partnership we can form is with Him. "If God is for us, who can be against us?" (Rom. 8:31).

Messages of the Four Winds

Many see the number four as signifying totality, a finishing point. There are four winds; four cardinal directions; four headwaters out of Eden; four seasons in our modern year; four evangelists, in the four Gospels; and in Revelation 7:1 "four angels standing at the four corners of the earth, holding back the four winds of the earth to prevent any wind from blowing on the land or on the sea or on any tree." This is an image of God's protection through Jesus.

Scripture continually reminds us that God is always in control, even of the wind. Consider Exodus 10:13 and Exodus 10:19, which tell us that God made the east wind carry the locusts to Egypt, and the west wind blew them away. God was in control. He set events in motion to redeem His people. God's power is described again in Psalm 78:26: "He let loose the east wind from the heavens and by his power made the south wind blow."

Ecclesiastes 1:6 provides a poetic description of the never-ending nature of God's love for us: "The wind blows to the south and turns to the north; round and round it goes, ever returning on its course." And Proverbs 30:4 tells us the identity of the wind's gatherer: "Who has gone up to heaven and come down? Whose hands have gathered up the wind? Who has wrapped up the waters in a cloak? Who has established all the ends of the earth? What is his name, and what is the name of his son? Surely you know!"

Cherubim on Gentle Breezes

Psalm 18 is David's song of gratitude to God for rescuing him from his enemies and from Saul. David describes God as his rock, his fortress, his deliverer, his salvation, his stronghold. Read Psalm 18:10: "He mounted the cherubim and flew; he soared on the wings of the wind" to come to David's rescue.

Cherubim are mighty angelic beings. They are God's attendants and guardians. Genesis 3:24 says that God stationed a cherubim as guardian of Eden's tree of life. Cherubim were also symbolic guardians of the Most Holy Place (Ex. 26:31-33). Read Exodus 25:18-22 and imagine the protective cherubim, with wings outstretched, on the ark of the covenant.

Close your eyes and picture God as David describes Him, soaring on the wind's wings to stand beside you. Whatever today throws at you, remember that the God who protected David is the God who protects you.

Feathered Friends and Gusty Gales

Jesus spent much of His ministry teaching people to love God and love others; but equally important, Jesus wants us to love ourselves. Loving ourselves honors the One who created us and enables us to love others. Read Matthew 6: 25, 26: "Is not life more than food, and the body more than clothes? Look at the birds of the air; they do not sow or reap or store away in barns, and yet your heavenly Father feeds them. Are you not much more valuable than they?" Jesus conveys the idea that God values and nurtures us with quiet strength.

God's presence can also feel strong and commanding. "When the day of Pentecost came, they were all together in one place. Suddenly a sound like the blowing of a violent wind came from heaven and filled the whole house where they were sitting" (Acts 2:1, 2). The apostle Luke tells us that God's power, mighty and forceful, literally blew into the meeting place of those following Jesus. The Holy Spirit, as a powerful wind, was present with God's people that day.

Experience the excitement that Luke and his friends felt. God was with them! Jesus lives! They felt Him! They heard Him! As you step into your day, step outside your comfort zone and be confident that God is with you. Rejoice!

Life Storms

Imagine a day in the life of the disciples. This day, as usual, Jesus attracted a big crowd. But today the press of people was so great that Jesus stepped into a boat and let it drift out onto the water. There the disciples sat and listened to Jesus explain parable after parable to the large crowd on the shore. They tried to soak in His words. They tried to grasp the magnitude of His teachings. By evening Jesus needed rest, and the disciples steered the boat across the lake.

"A furious squall came up, and the waves broke over the boat, so that it was nearly swamped. Jesus was in the stern, sleeping on a cushion. The disciples woke him and said to him, 'Teacher, don't you care if we drown?' He got up, rebuked the wind and said to the waves, 'Quiet! Be still!' Then the wind died down and it was completely calm. He said to his disciples, 'Why are you so afraid? Do you still have no faith?' They were terrified and asked each other, 'Who is this? Even the wind and the waves obey him!' " (Mark 4:37-41).

Put yourself in the disciples' boat. They feared that the storm was going to sink the boat and they would drown, but they were even more terrified when Jesus calmed the storm. Who *was* this man sleeping on a cushion in their boat?

Read Psalm 107:23-32. Who calms the storm in this song of praise?

Jesus demonstrated His divine power over nature by calming the storm, and He called His disciples to understand the power of their own faith. Because of their faith in Jesus, the disciples had the power to declare peace to the storm, too.

What storms of life do you face today? In John 14:18 Jesus says, "I will not leave you all alone . . . ; I will come back to you" (NCV). The One who was present with the disciples is here with you and me. When life's storms rear their heads, call on His name. Trust Him to answer. Exercise your own faith.

Prayer Focus

Dear God, thank You for the messages You carry to us on the wind. Thank You for the storms of life that teach us lessons, the gentle breezes that nudge us in the right direction, for the days we feel as light as a feather, and most of all, for being present with us through it all. We call on Your holy name in gratitude for all You have done, all You do, and all that You will do. Amen.

Zoom Lens

Read Acts 27 about the apostle Paul's perilous sea journey to Rome. What strong winds did Paul encounter in Acts 27:14? In verses 22 through 24 notice the strength and steadiness Paul gleaned from God's presence. Paul's faith in God reminds us of Psalm 46:10: "Be still, and know that I am God."

Action Shot

Read Job 12:10. In whose hand is the breath of all humankind? Sit outside and simply listen to the wind. Is it calm and peaceful, whispering? Is it strong and forceful?

King Solomon reminds us of the peace God wills for us in being content with what comes in life: "Better one handful with tranquillity than two handfuls with toil and chasing after the wind" (Eccl. 4:6).

Take a few minutes today to sit quietly and simply focus on your inhales and exhales, the breath of life that God placed in you.

Chapter 14

Water: Liquid Light

A river watering the garden flowed from Eden; from there it was separated into four headwaters.
—Genesis 2:10

Water is one of life's greatest necessities and deepest mysteries. Genesis 1:2 says, "Now the earth was formless and empty, darkness was over the surface of the deep, and the Spirit of God was hovering over the waters." As God created the earth, the waters separated and filled with living creatures. Water turns earth's grass green and hydrates the soil. Water gives life and takes life. Water cleanses, purifies, replenishes, restores. Water is substantial, whether it trickles gently along a streambed or surges in a violent flood.

"Deep calls to deep in the roar of your waterfalls; all your waves and breakers have swept over me" (Ps. 42:7).

In water the flow of life rises and falls.

A stream of running water is a symbol for the living water of God. Psalm 46:4, 5 says, "There is a river whose streams make glad the city of God, the holy place where the Most High dwells. God is within her, she will not fall; God will help her at break of day."

Water is a symbol of rescue and healing for Bible characters in both the Old and New Testaments. Author J. C. Cooper explains, "Water is the liquid counterpart of light."

With Jesus as the light of the world, stories of water illuminate our paths.

Read 2 Kings 5. The prophet Elisha told Naaman to dunk himself in the Jordan River to cure his leprosy. How many times did Naaman have to dip under the water to be healed?

Water Crossings

Read Exodus 2:1-10, a Bible story in which water unites and protects people who come from two different backgrounds. What did Pharaoh's daughter name the baby that she "drew out of the water"?

God used water as a means to protect that baby, who grew up into a man. Read the story of the parting of the Red Sea, found in Exodus 14. Moses and the Israelites were fleeing from Pharaoh and the Egyptians toward the Promised Land. They reached the Red Sea and came to a screeching halt because they could neither cross it nor go around it. But God was not going to leave them hanging; He would fulfill His promise to free them and give them their own land to live on. With a strong wind and Moses' cooperation, God pushed all the water to both sides so that a path of dry ground lay before the Israelites. They proceeded to cross the Red Sea and made it safely to the other side; however, the Egyptians, who thought they could simply follow the Israelites across, perished in the sea because God closed the waters in on them to prevent them from catching up. The Israelites, now on the other side of the Red Sea and safe from the Egyptians who were pursuing them, were beginning a new chapter in their lives.Crossing a body of water symbolizes a change from one state to another. For the Israelites, the flight from Egypt transformed them from slavery to freedom. The former captives were now free to follow and obey their God.

Recall the story of Elijah departing Elisha in 2 Kings 2:1-14. Elisha crossed the river Jordan, first as Elijah's servant. But he returned as a prophet with his request granted—a double portion of Elijah's spirit.

Hidden Water

Would you be amazed to see water gush from a rock? Imagine the Israelites traveling through the dry, desolate desert after their exodus from Egypt. When camping at a place called Rephidim where there was no water, they blamed Moses for their trouble. "Why did you bring us up out of Egypt to make us and our children . . . die of thirst?" they demanded (see Ex. 17:3).

"What am I to do with these people?" Moses asked the Lord, and God told him to take his staff and strike a certain rock (Ex. 17:4-6). "I will stand there before you by the rock at Horeb," the Lord told Moses, and enough water gushed from the rock to quench the thirst of the thousands of people and their animals.

Psalm 105:41 echoes the story: "He opened the rock, and water gushed out; it flowed like a river in the desert."

Think about the image of water gushing from a rock as God pours out His help and blessings for you and me through Jesus.

You'll find a similar story of God's provision for the Israelites in Exodus 15:22-27. After traveling three dusty days with no water, the Israelites found water in Marah, but it was so bitter they couldn't drink it. They complained to Moses, who looked to

God for help. God pointed out a nearby stick and told Moses to throw it into the water. The water immediately turned fresh, ready to quench the thirst of the thousands of people.

The Holy Land's climate makes water a precious commodity. Our bodies are approximately 80 percent water, and the three days that the Israelites traveled without water is on the outer limits of time that a human being can survive without water. The Israelites surely craved water, not only for drinking but for ritual purification as well. Cleansing the body with water is symbolic of cleansing the spirit by following Jesus.

Baptismal Waters

When John the Baptist baptized Jesus, Jesus rose up out of the water, the heavens opened, the Holy Spirit descended on Him, and God claimed Him as His Son. John says that Jesus' disciples baptized followers (John 4:2), and Peter explains baptism in 1 Peter 3:21: "This water symbolizes baptism that now saves you also—not the removal of dirt from the body but the pledge of a clear conscience toward God. It saves you by the resurrection of Jesus Christ."

For Jesus, baptism was a rite of passage, a renewal and regeneration, the starting point of His ministry. For us, baptism by water is an initiation into God's family. When we are baptized, God claims us through our belief in Jesus. For us, baptism cleanses the old and gives birth to the new. It is a symbol of our pledge to follow Christ.

Fountain of Life

The water well was the community meeting place in Bible times. Each day people carried large clay jars to the well, filled them, and then carried them home to their families. Isaiah 12:3 says, "With joy you will draw water from the wells of salvation." Jacob first met his true love, Rachel, at a well where she drew water for her father's sheep (Gen. 29:10).

John 4:1-26 tells the story of Jesus' conversation with a Samaritan woman. Traveling to Galilee, Jesus and His disciples went to the town of Sychar, in Samaria, "near the plot of ground Jacob had given to his son Joseph." Jesus was tired, so He sat down to rest at Jacob's well while His disciples continued farther to buy food for them to eat. Around noon, a Samaritan woman came to the well, and Jesus asked her to draw a drink for Him. The Samaritan woman was surprised that a Jewish man would speak to her.

Jesus told her that she should ask Him for living water so that she would never thirst again, water that would become "a spring of water welling up to eternal life" inside the person who drank it. Jesus, the fountain of life, echoes this scripture: "The Lord will guide you always; he will satisfy your needs in a sun-scorched land and will strengthen your frame. You will be like a well-watered garden, like a spring whose waters never fail" (Isa. 58:11).

Bethlehem's Well

Read 2 Samuel 23:13-17. When David was encamped at the cave of Adullam, he was homesick and wished out loud for a drink from his father's well in Bethlehem. Unbeknown to David, three of his mightiest warriors heard his wish and risked their lives to get the water for him. David was humbled by their loyalty but refused to drink the water. He told them that only God deserves such devotion and then offered the water as a sacrifice to God.

Waiting at the Water

John 5:1-9 records the story of a paralytic man's healing. Near the Sheep Gate in Jerusalem are the pools of Bethesda, framed by "five covered colonnades." In 1956 archaeologists unearthed the remains of Bethesda, including segments of the five covered colonnades. People still visit this site and rejoice in the healing that took place there.

John explains that it was believed that occasionally an angel stirred the pool's waters. At those times, the people believed, the waters could heal. People who were blind, lame, or paralyzed tried to be the first to get into the pool for their chance to be healed. One lame man had stayed near the Bethesda pools for 38 years but was never able to get into the waters in time.

Jesus saw this man and asked him, "Do you want to get well?"

"The invalid replied, 'I have no one to help me into the pool when the water is stirred. While I am trying to get in, someone else goes down ahead of me.' "

Listen to verses 8 and 9: "Then Jesus said to him, 'Get up! Pick up your mat and walk.' At once the man was cured; he picked up his mat and walked. The day on which this took place was a Sabbath."

Imagine standing up near the sacred waters you'd longed to bathe in for 38 years and suddenly realizing those waters weren't even necessary! Jesus' words sufficed.

Maybe there are problems in your life that you'd like to change. Don't wait. Take them to Jesus today.

Tears of Gratitude

Read Luke 7:36-50. Jesus was visiting a Pharisee's home, when a woman silently entered, knelt down at His feet, and washed them with her tears. Her act was one of reverence, humility, and gratitude. Scripture says that the woman had sinned greatly but that Jesus had forgiven her and taken away that sin.

By washing Jesus' feet with her tears, this woman seemed to wash away the guilt and pain of her past. Being forgiven by Jesus helped the woman put her faith completely in her Lord.

The Nerve of Peter

Matthew 14 tells us that when Jesus learned of John the Baptist's death, He was so sad that He wanted to go away for a while and be alone. But the crowds followed Him. His compassion led Him to heal the sick and perform the miraculous feeding of the five thousand. Later that evening Jesus climbed the hillside to pray alone. His disciples were in a boat on the Sea of Galilee, far away from land, and Jesus wanted to join them.

"Shortly before dawn," the disciples saw Jesus "walking on the lake . . . [and] were terrified." They thought that they were looking at a ghost, so Jesus gently calmed their fears right away and told them it was He and that they need not be afraid. " 'Lord, if it's you,' Peter replied, 'tell me to come to you on the water.' 'Come,' he said. Then Peter got down out of the boat, walked on the water and came toward Jesus. But when he saw the wind, he was afraid and, beginning to sink, cried out, 'Lord, save me!' " Jesus immediately reached out to Peter and kept him from going under. Then Jesus said, "You of little faith . . . why did you doubt?" Marveling at what they had just witnessed, the disciples declared, "Truly you are the Son of God" (Matt. 14:25-33).

We aren't told if all 12 disciples—Matthew, Simon, Philip, James, John, James the brother of John, Andrew, Bartholomew, Thomas, Judas, Judas Iscariot, and Simon Peter—were in the boat, but of those who were present, only Peter dared to leave it. Yes, Peter got scared, and yes, he began to sink under the waves. But he had the courage to step off the boat! And who was there to hold his hand when he sank? Jesus!

You and I can step off our own boats today. We can step out in faith. We can be bold and try something new. We can reach out a hand in friendship. We can apply for a new job. We can ask for the help we need. We can offer help to others. Let's begin by asking Jesus to increase our faith, and then let's step off the boat!

The King Serves

Read John 13:1-17. Imagine the disciples gathering for this important meal with Jesus. They'd traveled in the sandy, gritty climate of the Holy Land in sandals. Their feet were sweaty and dirty. The task of washing a guest's feet usually fell to the lowliest servant in the household, but there was no one available to do the job. Picture the disciples' awkward glances. Imagine them staring at the walls to avoid one another's eyes. Jesus knew these friends well. Jesus and the 12 men were as close as brothers, and He knew their hearts and minds.

Jesus stood up from the table, tied a towel around His waist, and poured water into a basin. Then, one by one, He washed the feet of each disciple and dried them with the towel wrapped around His waist. Apparently no one balked until Jesus reached Simon Peter.

"Jesus, You are my Lord," Peter objected. "You can't wash my feet." But Jesus insisted and told Peter that someday he would understand why.

After Jesus washed the feet of every one of His disciples, He asked: "Do you understand what I have done for you? You call me 'Teacher' and 'Lord,' and rightly so, for that is what I am. Now that I, your Lord and Teacher, have washed your feet, you also should wash one another's feet. I have set you an example that you should do as I have done for you. Very truly I tell you, no servant is greater than his master, nor is a messenger greater than the one who sent him. Now that you know these things, you will be blessed if you do them" (John 13:12-17).

Notice that Jesus didn't tell them to serve one another because it was the law, because it was what God expected, or because it was the right thing to do. Jesus told them to serve one another because "you will be blessed if you do."

Have you ever noticed that when you give to others from your heart, you are as blessed as the person who receives your gift?

Do a random act of kindness today. If possible, keep it a secret.

The First Sign: Saving the Best for Last

John 2 describes the first sign that Jesus' ministry was headed in a glorious direction. Jesus, His family, and His disciples were attending a wedding in Cana, Galilee. Everyone was enjoying the festivities when suddenly the wine being served ran out. Jesus' mother, expecting her Son to intervene in the situation somehow, brought the issue to Jesus' attention. Jesus' answer to her was "Why do you involve me? . . . My hour has not yet come." Sensing, however, that Jesus was nonetheless about to do something about the depleted wine, Mary told the servants, "Do whatever he tells you." Pointing to the "six stone water jars, the kind used by the Jews for ceremonial washing," Jesus instructed the servants to fill them with water and to "draw some out and take it to the master of the banquet," which the servants did. Then the master, not realizing what Jesus and the servants had just done, tasted the water—which now was wine. Impressed with its taste, the master said to the bridegroom, "Everyone brings out the choice wine first and then the cheaper wine after the guests have had too much to drink; but you have saved the best till now." The miracle Jesus performed at the wedding in Cana was significant because "it was the first of the signs through which he revealed his glory," and it instilled faith and belief in His disciples (verses 4, 5, 10, 11).

The apostle John, a master of symbolic writing, called the event in Cana not a miracle but a "sign" of Jesus' glory. As Jesus transformed water into wine, He came to transform our lives, through His glory. In John 10:10 Jesus says, "I came that they may have life, and may have it abundantly" (ASV). As Jesus transformed the water not into ordinary wine, but into the *best* wine, Jesus wants to transform our lives in miraculous ways.

Notice the symbolism in the vessels that Jesus uses in the story. These jars were usually used for ceremonial washing, to carry out the Jewish law and custom. Jesus' intent is to transform something good, God's law, into something even better. Jesus guides people to God "above and beyond" the sake of the law: He wants to show followers the sheer joy they can experience every day in living for God.

Ask God what type of vessel He wants you to be and how He wants your spirit to be transformed. Being obedient to God's laws isn't dull and boring. Jesus calls us to live abundantly, to be constantly made fresh and new in Him. When we live for Jesus, we enjoy life. Every day is a new adventure. Consider what Paul wrote: "Do not conform to the pattern of this world, but be transformed by the renewing of your mind" (Rom. 12:2).

Prayer Focus

Dear God, thank You for the gift of water that heals and transforms us body, mind, and spirit. Help us to live as Jesus lives and do as Jesus does, knowing we will be blessed if we do! Thank You for blessing us abundantly and for renewing us day by day. Amen.

Zoom Lens

Read Isaiah 44:1-3: "But now listen, Jacob, my servant, Israel, whom I have chosen. This is what the Lord says—he who made you, who formed you in the womb, and who will help you: Do not be afraid, Jacob, my servant, Jeshurun, whom I have chosen. For I will pour water on the thirsty land, and streams on the dry ground; I will pour out my Spirit on your offspring, and my blessing on your descendants." The God of Jacob is our God. Thank Him for His blessings today.

Action Shot

Read Psalm 63:1: "You, God, are my God, earnestly I seek you; I thirst for you, my whole being longs for you, in a dry and parched land where there is no water."

If you're able, visit a body of water today—a stream, lake, ocean, or swimming pool—or simply fill a bowl with water. Immerse yourself, or touch the water, and ask God to heal any part of you, mind, body, or spirit, that needs healing. Invite Jesus to be your anchor in the waters of life.

Chapter 15

Fire: Sparks of Faith

The Lord went ahead of them . . . in a pillar of fire to give them light.
—Exodus 13:21

When we imagine purifying, illuminating, cleansing fire, we can think of God as the spark of our soul. It was through a burning bush that the Lord got Moses' attention and commissioned him for his divine assignment (Ex. 3), and John the Baptist predicted that Jesus would baptize with fire and the Holy Spirit. The Bible's fiery stories, flickering like flames and dancing like rays of light, bring us courage and passion to move in the right direction, to blaze the straight and narrow trails in our lives.

Read 1 Kings 18. When the followers of Baal could not summon fire, which prophet of God called on Him to send down fire with these words: "Lord, the God of Abraham, Isaac and Israel, let it be known today that you are God in Israel and that I am your servant and have done all these things at your command. Answer me, Lord, answer me, so these people will know that you, Lord, are God, and that you are turning their hearts back again" (1 Kings 18:36, 37).

A Bush on Fire

One day Moses was in the middle of taking care of his father-in-law's sheep, leading them to "the far side of the wilderness." When he arrived at "Horeb, the mountain of God" . . . "the angel of the Lord appeared to him in flames of fire from within a bush. Moses saw that though the bush was on fire it did not burn up. So Moses thought, 'I will go over and see this strange sight—why the bush does not burn up.' When the Lord saw that he had gone over to look, God called to him from within the bush, 'Moses! Moses!' And Moses said, 'Here I am' " (Ex. 3:1-4).

Surely God succeeded in arresting Moses' attention and solemnly announcing his mission through the mysterious fiery bush. As you read the next story, keep in mind that Moses said yes to God.

When God Called Isaiah

Isaiah 6:1-8 describes that one day the man Isaiah was given a vision and "saw the Lord, high and exalted, seated on a throne." He also noticed some intriguing seraphim who were extolling the holiness and glory of God. The imagery becomes more dramatic—and smoky! "At the sound of their voices the doorposts and thresholds shook and the temple was filled with smoke." However, overwhelmed with what he just saw, Isaiah cried out, "Woe to me! . . . I am ruined! For I am a man of unclean lips, and I live among a people of unclean lips, and my eyes have seen the King, the Lord Almighty." God's goodness and glory in the vision struck Isaiah so profoundly that it brought him to despair when he considered how infinitely it contrasted with human nature. But God did not let Isaiah dwell in that despair. One of the seraphim took a hot coal, touched Isaiah's mouth with it, and said, "See, this has touched your lips; your guilt is taken away and your sin atoned for." And when God asked the seraphim, "Whom shall I send? And who will go for us?" Isaiah, without hesitation, spoke up and said, "Here am I. Send me!"

Here I Am

When God called, what did both Moses and Isaiah answer?

Neither Moses nor Isaiah felt worthy of God's faith in them, but each received a fiery sign that God was calling him. God may not appear to you and me in a burning bush. He may not send an angel to cleanse our lips with a fiery coal and tell us we are forgiven the way He did for Isaiah. But God calls our names nonetheless. He has faith in us.

Today, in the ordinary tasks of life, we can answer as Moses and Isaiah did, "Here I am, Lord!"

I AM WHO I AM

Scholars have tried to guess what kind of bush Moses saw burning, but no one knows for sure. It might have been a thorny acacia bush, a gas plant, the crimson-flowered mistletoe, or some other shrub.

After Moses said, "Here I am," God told him to lead His people out of Egypt.

"Moses said to God, 'Suppose I go to the Israelites and say to them, "The God of your fathers has sent me to you," and they ask me, "What is his name?" Then what shall I tell them?' God said to Moses, 'I AM WHO I AM. This is what you are to say to the Israelites: "I AM has sent me to you"'" (Ex. 3:13, 14).

In the book of John, Jesus, claiming His divinity as the Son of God, repeats "I am" in seven different ways:

"I am the bread of life" (John 6:35, 48).

"I am the light of the world" (John 8:12; 9:5).

"I am the gate" (John 10:7, 9).

"I am the good shepherd" (John 10:11, 14).

"I am the resurrection and the life" (John 11:25).

"I am the way and the truth and the life" (John 14:6).

"I am the true vine" (John 15:1).

In *Number in Scripture* Ethelbert W. Bullinger explains (as do many Bible scholars) that the meaning of the number 7 is "perfection" and "completeness."

The Long Route Home

Read Exodus 13:17-22. After God called Moses through the burning bush to liberate the Israelites from Egypt, He led them not the short way through the land of the Philistines, but "around by the desert road toward the Red Sea." Scripture says that God guided their journey as a cloud during the day and by fire at night. Verse 22 says that God was with them always: "Neither the pillar of cloud by day nor the pillar of fire by night left its place in front of the people."

One of the psalms echoes the story of the Israelites being saved by God. "He spread out a cloud as a covering, and a fire to give light at night" (Ps. 105:39).

Have you ever prayed for a visible answer from God? The Israelites received the blessing of a visual sign from God. Many fires in nature are uncontrolled, consuming everything in their path. The Israelites' pillar of fire overhead was protective and intentionally controlled by God. The cloud showed them where to walk during the day; the pillar of fire led their way at night. If they needed to stay put, the cloud or pillar didn't budge.

Since the Israelites were on the run from their enemies in unfamiliar territory, God's definite direction surely must have been comforting. God may not send us a cloud or a pillar of fire, but He guides us just the same. When we spend time talking and listening to God each day, He may provide a different kind of sign or a gentle nudge that we feel in our hearts. He is sure to lead us in the right direction, even if that direction means we have to take the long route.

A Fiery Message

In the book of Numbers we witness the Israelites facing the rough, open wilderness. They were disheartened by their having to wander in the desert of the Sinai Peninsula and therefore wandered away from God. They lost their faith.

"Now the people complained about their hardships in the hearing of the Lord, and when he heard them his anger was aroused. Then fire from the Lord burned among them and consumed some of the outskirts of the camp. When the people cried out to Moses, he prayed to the Lord and the fire died down. So that place was called Taberah, because fire from the Lord had burned among them" (Num. 11:1-3).

At times fires can be destructive, destroying homes or property. Wildfires can destroy many acres of land or forest. But fires can also melt and transform old materials into something new and useful. When a tree dies, the brush can be burned to reduce the dead branches to ashes, which can be returned to the earth to enrich the soil. Fires can purge, purify, and cleanse. In the fiery message that God sent the Israelites, He used fire to refine their ideas and transform their faith. Read Isaiah 48:10: "See, I have refined you, though not as silver; I have tested you in the furnace of affliction."

God remained faithful to the Israelites throughout their trials, and He remains faithful to us today. How has God's love refined your faith?

Words as Fire: Spark Control

Sometimes we wish words were hooks on the end of a fishing rod that we could just reel back in. Words slip from our mouths that we wish we had never spoken. Jesus' own brother James offers this insight. "When we put bits into the mouths of horses to make them obey us, we can turn the whole animal. Or take ships as an example. Although they are so large and are driven by strong winds, they are steered by a very small rudder wherever the pilot wants to go. Likewise, the tongue is a small part of the body, but it makes great boasts. Consider what a great forest is set on fire by a small spark" (James 3:3-5).

Do you ever get in trouble because of your tongue? Do you ever speak first and think later? The first step toward "taming your tongue" is to pay attention to the words you speak today. If you hurt someone, use your tongue to mend the hurt. Apologize.

If you realize that you talked when you should have been silent, be quieter next time. If you let someone be bad-mouthed while you stood by and said nothing, make a decision that you'll never do that again.

Blaze a Trail Through the Narrow Gate

Fire is symbolic of courage and passion. Luke reminds us of the fervor he felt in the presence of the resurrected Jesus: "Were not our hearts burning within us while he talked with us on the road and opened the Scriptures to us?" (Luke 24:32).

In Matthew 7:13, 14 Jesus shows us the path we should follow: "Enter through the narrow gate. For wide is the gate and broad is the road that leads to destruction, and many enter through it. But small is the gate and narrow the road that leads to life, and only a few find it." Jesus carved the pathway. His disciples were the first to follow. Our job is to blaze a trail behind them.

Luke gives us a glimpse of the early Christian church in the book of Acts. Read Luke's account of the Holy Spirit's presence with the disciples in Acts 2:3, 4: "They saw what seemed to be tongues of fire that separated and came to rest on each of them. All of them were filled with the Holy Spirit and began to speak in other tongues as the Spirit enabled them."

They were amazed that while they gathered together to worship, people spoke in different languages "about the wonderful things God has done" (Acts 2:11, NLT).

What has God done in your life, or in the lives of your family and friends? Are you fired up about the wonderful things God has done? Today, live your life with Christ-centered passion.

Prayer Focus

Dear God, thank You for the mystery of fire and for kindling Your flame within us. We are forever grateful to feel the spark of Your divinity in our lives. Ignite our faith and help us to shine light on another's path today. Amen.

Zoom Lens

Light a candle and read Daniel 3. Shadrach, Meshach, and Abednego refused to worship King Nebuchadnezzar's statue because they wanted to be true to God's command to worship only Him. How did God protect these three from fire?

Action Shot

The author of Psalm 39:3 wrote, "My heart grew hot within me. While I meditated, the fire burned." If you can do so safely, build a small fire outside today. Be still and gaze at the dancing flames.

Ask God to illuminate the direction you should take today.

Section Five

Bible Skylights: The Sun, Moon, and Stars

Praise him, sun and moon; praise him, all you shining stars.
—Psalm 148:3

Chapter 16

The Sun: Hope and Abundance

The path of the righteous is like the morning sun, shining ever brighter till the full light of day.
—Proverbs 4:18

Imagine you're living in the year 1543. It was "well known" by the learned people that Planet Earth is the center of the universe; the sun and other planets were thought to revolve around us!

Then doctor, mathematician, and part-time astronomer Nicolaus Copernicus published a book, *On the Revolutions of the Celestial Spheres*, which turned the then-known world upside down. Copernicus' heliocentric theory suggested instead that our sun is the center of our solar system around which the earth and the other planets revolve.

We know today that Copernicus was correct. The sun *is* the center of our universe. We also know that the sun is simply a bright star. Our sun's temperature measures about 10,472°F (5,800°C) and provides the earth with life-giving light and heat. We are able to live on the earth because of the sun's energy, but the sun is also an indescribable source of beauty and wonder. When we walk through a dense forest, we gaze at the columns of light that filter through the boughs of the trees. Bodies of water catch the sun's reflection. The sun's light paints the clouds and sky at sunrise and sunset and casts shadows in myriad forms.

Read Exodus 16:21. When God sent manna for the Israelites, at what time of day did it melt away? Let's spotlight other Bible tales of the radiant, life-giving beacon in our sky.

Sun of Righteousness

The sun is a reminder of God's abundance; its light is available to everyone, never excludes, and shines anew each morning. Everything that God created, including the sun, bears some attribute of His because He is its Creator.

There are many Scripture verses that speak of God as the one who created the sun. Psalm 74:16 reminds us, "The day is yours . . . you established the sun." You can also read the Creation account in Genesis 1 and search for the verses that speak about God creating the sun. People often take for granted that they will wake to a "rising" sun, and yet the Bible tells us that even the sun cannot do its duty without God's sustaining power. The book of Colossians says that "in him [Jesus Christ] all things were created: things in heaven and on earth, visible and invisible, whether thrones or powers or rulers or authorities; all things have been created through him and for him. He is before all things, and in him all things hold together" (Col. 1:16, 17). Hebrews 1:3 states that He "upholds the universe by his power" (ESV).

Have you ever thought about the fact that the same sun that Jesus looked up to see when He lived on earth is the one that you and I see in the morning when we rise? Our lives are short and miniscule compared to the sun's tireless existence, which, as we read, is upheld by God Himself. Maybe this is why Solomon used the phrase "under the sun" so frequently when writing Ecclesiastes—to remind us how small and fragile we are and how desperately we need God and His purpose in our lives.

Even though the sun in itself is not eternal, people have ascribed to it this attribute and compared it with God's own nature; hear the psalmist's wish: "May he endure as long as the sun . . . through all generations" (Ps. 72:5). The beautiful psalms offer the hopeful message that God and His love will endure forever, as long as the sun. Read Psalm 72:17: "May his name endure forever; may it continue as long as the sun. Then all nations will be blessed through him, and they will call him blessed."

Jesus, the light of the world, includes the sun among His many names. The prophet Malachi illuminates the promise Jesus holds for us: "For you who revere my name, the sun of righteousness will rise with healing in its rays" (Mal. 4:2). Jesus is also called "the rising sun" who "will come to us from heaven to shine on those living in darkness and in the shadow of death, to guide our feet into the path of peace" (Luke 1:78, 79). Revelation 21:23 tells us that God's Holy City "does not need the sun or the moon to shine on it, for the glory of God gives it light, and the Lamb is its lamp."

Light Givers

While the Bible uses the image and characteristics of the sun to reflect back on our everlasting God, it intriguingly also uses such images to describe the mission and inheritance of God's people: "He will make your righteous reward shine like the dawn, your vindication like the noonday sun" (Ps. 37:6); and "the path of the righteous is like the morning sun, shining ever brighter till the full light of day" (Prov. 4:18).

Matthew 5:14-16 says, "You are the light of the world . . . let your light shine before others." As the sun is the source of our light on the earth, the apostle Luke, whose name means "light," included Jesus' reminder to let our lights shine. "No one lights a lamp and puts it in a place where it will be hidden, or under a bowl. Instead they put it on its stand, so that those who come in may see the light" (Luke 11:33). The point for a source of light is to shine, and Jesus likewise wants the light that He has placed within us to shine so that others can connect with Him, the Light of the world. And 1 John 1:7 reminds us, "If we walk in the light, as he is in the light, we have fellowship with one another."

The Sun's White Light

Read Psalm 113:3: "From the rising of the sun to the place where it sets, the name of the Lord is to be praised."

While we protect our eyes by not looking directly at the sun, sunrise and sunset offer us glorious opportunities to gaze at the miraculous spectacles in the sky. We often imagine God using broad brushstrokes to paint new sky images throughout the day and night, but there is a scientific explanation for the mind-blowing colors we see at sunrise and sunset.

The sun *looks* yellow during the day, but invisible, white light shines inside the sun. White light contains every color in the rainbow. If you hold a prism up to the sun, you can reflect the colors onto a wall. Red has the longest wavelength, followed by orange, yellow, green, blue, indigo, and violet.

The atmosphere around the earth is made of gas molecules, such as the oxygen we breathe and nitrogen. During the day, sunlight streams into the earth's atmosphere, and zooming gas molecules work like cheese graters. As white light passes through, gas molecules grate the white into all the colors, and they scatter in slivers. Earth's atmosphere is a huge prism bending the colors in white light in different directions. The blue tones, with short wavelengths, scatter first. Imagine yourself swimming in a lake. You scatter the small waves close to you, but you don't affect the larger waves far away. As blue wavelengths flood the sky during the day, the sunlight loses its blue tone, and the sun appears yellow.

When the sun is low in the sky at sunrise and sunset, white light treks a farther trail through the atmosphere than when the sun is overhead during the day. Most of the short, blue tones are scattered across the sky. Radiant sunsets are created when the colors with the longest wavelengths—red and orange—scatter on the horizon. If the air near the ground is thick with dust or pollution, orange, pink, and red light are more likely to scatter, with brilliant effects. On a clear day, the sunrise or sunset can be simply yellow. Our sky looks different each day because the gas, smoke, water vapor, ice crystals, and pollution in the earth's atmosphere constantly scatter the prism of white light in a unique way.

Sunrise, Sunset, and Jesus' Ministry

The times of sunrise and sunset play a role in Jesus' life and resurrection. Read Mark 1 to reexperience the beginning of Jesus' ministry. Feel the disciples' excitement. Experience the transformation Jesus brought in people's lives as He taught the good news and healed the sick. Mark 1:32 tells us that many healings took place one Sabbath evening, "after sunset," when "the people brought to Jesus all the sick and demon-possessed." That Jesus performed these healings at sunset is significant. As the sun went down, Jesus released people from the parts of their lives that weighed down their spirits. Jesus helped them surrender their burdens as the sun surrendered its light.

The Transfiguration

Read Luke 9:1-20. After the 5,000 were fed, Jesus went away to pray. When His disciples joined Him, Jesus stood up and asked a staggering question: "Who do you say I am?"

Imagine the intensity of His gaze as He stood face to face with His disciples.

"Who do you say I am?"

Peter's answer breaks the silence: "God's Messiah."

"About eight days after Jesus said this, he took Peter, John and James with him and went up onto a mountain to pray. As he was praying, the appearance of his face changed, and his clothes became as bright as a flash of lightning. Two men, Moses and Elijah, appeared in glorious splendor, talking with Jesus" (Luke 9:28-30). This event is known as the Transfiguration. Some scholars believe that Jesus' transfiguration occurred on Mount Tabor, others Mount Hermon. The parallel passage, in Matthew 17:2, describes the moment of Jesus' transfiguration this way: "His face shone like the sun, and his clothes became as white as the light."

It reminds us of the powerful words of Psalm 84:11: "For the Lord God is a sun and shield; the Lord bestows favor and honor; no good thing does he withhold from those whose walk is blameless."

Who do *you* say Jesus is?

Today let's stand face to face with Jesus, declaring as Peter did, "God's Messiah." Let's walk with Jesus, confident the Lord is our sun and our shield.

The Tomb at Sunrise

Imagine the unspeakable sadness of the three women who were going to care for Jesus' body after His death, as recorded in Mark 16: "When the Sabbath was over, Mary Magdalene, Mary the mother of James, and Salome bought spices so that they might go to anoint Jesus' body." It is fitting that these grieving, despondent women went to the tomb "very early on the first day of the week, just after sunrise" because they were going to be greeted by an angel with the best news ever: "You are looking for Jesus the Nazarene, who was crucified. He has risen! He is not here. See the place where they laid him. But go, tell his disciples and Peter, 'He is going ahead of you into Galilee. There you will see him, just as he told you'" (Mark 16:1, 2, 6, 7).

At first the three women tremble and are bewildered (verse 8), but not for long, for their unspeakable sadness turns to indescribable joy! Sunrise, a symbol of the newness of life, on this particular day brings an unbelievable new beginning.

When the Sun Stood Still

Psalm 104:19 says, "The sun knows when to go down," but Joshua 10 tells a story that defies scientific explanation. As you read, pay particular attention to Joshua 10:12-14: "On the day the Lord gave the Amorites over to Israel, Joshua said to the Lord in the presence of Israel: 'Sun, stand still over Gibeon, and you, moon, over the Valley of Aijalon.' So the sun stood still, and the moon stopped, till the nation avenged itself on its enemies, as it is written in the Book of Jashar. The sun stopped in the middle of the sky and delayed going down about a full day. There has never been a day like it before or since, a day when the Lord listened to a human being. Surely the Lord was fighting for Israel!"

Joshua was a mighty leader and a brave warrior, and in the midst of this great battle, he realized that the sun's light was fading. He was out of daylight. Most of us would say, "We gave it our best shot. Let's pack up, retreat, and get a good night's rest. We'll try again in the morning." But not Joshua; he simply asked God for more daylight!

Joshua, whose name means "Jehovah is salvation," trusted God to save him. Joshua believed in a God of power and might, a God who listens. Joshua believed in a God who is not defined by the laws of nature, but a God who controls them.

Joshua wanted to finish the job he set out to do, and he trusted God to come to his rescue. Joshua boldly asked for what he wanted and needed, and the Lord granted his wish!

Scripture proclaims that day as unique: "There has never been a day like it before or since."

Imagine the people standing under the mighty sun, and giving thanks to their generous and powerful God.

Today you and I can be as brave as Joshua. Whatever is on our hearts and minds, whatever we wish for or need, let's ask God about it. We live for a God of power and might. We live for a God who listens and rescues. We live for a God who is in control.

Prayer Focus

Dear God, thank You for Your glory; we see it shining in the light of the sun. As the sun's brilliant light illumines our sky, Your dazzling light fills our lives. We are grateful and joyful. We thank You for all the good things You bring to us today. Help us share Your goodness and abundance with others. Amen.

Zoom Lens

Read David's last words, recorded in 2 Samuel 23, especially verses 1 to 4. Watch the light of a morning sunrise on a cloudless morning. Think of the One who created it.

Action Shot

Psalm 96:2 tells us many ways to praise God: "Sing to the Lord, praise his name; proclaim his salvation day after day." We can honor God, and draw closer to Him, by praising Him every day of the week. You've probably guessed that human beings named Sunday after the sun, and on that day we can seize another opportunity to praise God for creating the glorious sun. We remember, though, that "from the rising of the sun to the place where it sets, the name of the Lord is to be praised" (Ps. 113:3).

Now read Psalm 19, a psalm of God's glory. Where did God pitch a tent for the sun (verse 4)? It's amazing that God's commands are called "radiant, giving light to the eyes" (verse 8). Write a psalm of your own that includes God's glorious creation of the sun and how His commands have brought light to your eyes.

Chapter 17

The Moon: Cycles of Life

He made the moon to mark the seasons.
—Psalm 104:19

Are you going through a phase?

When kids are 2 years old, and again when they're teenagers, parents often say, "They're just going through a phase." That simply means that the kid's behavior is less than desirable, but there's hope that he or she will outgrow it.

Adults also go through difficult phases in life. If you've read the book of Job, you may agree that Job spent the first half of his life in a phase. But despite his difficulties, Job continued to praise God's wonders, including one of His handiworks, the wondrous moon.

In Job 26:9 Job speaks of God's power to his friend Bildad, saying, "He covers the face of the full moon, spreading his clouds over it." Throughout recorded history people have observed the moon's phases with wonder. A mixture of beauty and mystery, the moon's rough, shadowy, crater-filled surface inspires our imagination. In times past, people sometimes thought they saw the face of a man in the moon.

Read Psalm 74. Who does Asaph say established the moon over the night? Let's explore other Bible stories of this moon that illumines the dark skies.

Observing the Moon's Silence

Read Psalm 136, a song of gratitude for all of God's works, including "the moon and stars to govern the night."

In 1609 Italian scientist Galileo Galilei was one of the first to get a closer look at the moon, the earth's only natural satellite, through the telescopes he constructed. Some planets have no moons, but the earth has one moon, Mars two, and (at last count) Neptune has 13 and Saturn 62. Our moon's diameter is about 2,000 miles, about one fourth of the earth's 8,000-mile diameter.

While the earth teems with life above ground, below ground, in the seas, and in the skies, our moon is bare and void of living things, water, air, or clouds. Our moon is a blend of rock and dust, its surface covered by craters, flat terrain, hills, valleys, and mountains.

Of the stars and planets that shine in the night sky, the moon's light appears brightest because it is closest to the earth, only 238,900 miles away. The moon actually sheds no light of its own but simply reflects the sun's light. In *A Natural History of the Senses* Diane Ackerman elaborates, "By day, if I held a mirror and bounced a spot of sunlight around the trees, I would be mimicking how the moon reflects light, having none of its own to give."

We always view the same side of the moon, but it appears different to us depending on the varying positions of the sun, moon, and earth.

From Darkness to Light

The changes we see in the moon are an essential part of our attraction to it. Many years ago people used the moon to help them keep track of the passage of time. The moon's cycles form a perfect, never-ending circle of transformation. Yet it hangs in the sky, still and steady like God's love. Its cycle, from complete darkness to complete light, symbolizes Jesus' victory over death and darkness.

The moon, like Jesus, signifies to us light in the darkness. Jesus said, "I am the light of the world. Whoever follows me will never walk in darkness, but will have the light of life" (John 8:12).

New Moons, Lunation, and the Lunar Calendar

In the Old Testament Moses transcribes God's instructions for ancient worship, including the New Moon feast: "Also at your times of rejoicing—your appointed festivals and New Moon feasts—you are to sound the trumpets over your burnt offerings and fellowship offerings, and they will be a memorial for you before your God. I am the Lord your God" (Num. 10:10).

The Latin word for moon is *luna*. It takes about one month (29½ days) for the moon to complete a lunation, a complete cycle of lunar phases from new moon to new moon. At new moon, the moon is almost precisely between the earth and the sun. At that point the sun illuminates the opposite side of the moon; we see the dark side of the moon.

On day 1 of lunation, the completely dark full moon waxes (the light reflected in the moon increases) toward a crescent moon, then the first-quarter moon (day 7).

As the first-quarter moon waxes to the completely illumined full moon, two weeks (14 or 15 days) have passed. The full moon wanes (the light reflected in the moon decreases) to the last-quarter moon (day 22), then a crescent moon, and finally another completely dark full moon (day 29½).

One cycle of the moon is about one month; a total of 12 moon cycles carries us through a calendar year. When our new year starts, many of us buy a printed calendar to hang on the wall, in which the days of the month are set at 28, 29, 30, or 31 days. When one month ends, we turn the page, and start a new month.

In Jesus' time the Jewish calendar was dictated by observing the moon's cycles. One month was the time it took for the lunar phases to cycle, new moon to new moon. Months (or "moonths," as the word was originally spelled) of the year were once called "moons."

The modern Jewish calendar is approximately 354 days, so an extra month is added about seven times every 19 years. In Bible times the barley fields helped dictate the calendar. The Passover, or feast of the barley harvest, could not be held until the barley was ripe. If farmers reported that the barley was not ready, the Jewish leaders added an extra month to the lunar calendar.

Moon Tides

If you've taken a trip to the beach (or if you're fortunate enough to live by the sea), you've observed the powerful and mysterious rise and fall of the ocean's water. The moon's gravity, combined with the gravitational pull of the sun and the earth's rotation, affects ocean tides. In most oceans there are two high tides and two low tides each day, but in some places there is one high and one low tide. We're reminded in Psalm 148:7 to "praise the Lord from the . . . ocean depths."

Moon Songs

In the hymn "All Creatures of Our God and King," Saint Francis of Assisi wrote: "O sister moon with silver gleam! O Praise Him!"* The way Saint Francis of Assisi observed the natural world as a canvas displaying God's character calls to mind Psalm 148, which similarly praises God's handiwork in the heavens: "Praise the Lord. Praise the Lord from the heavens; praise him in the heights above. Praise him, all his angels; praise him, all his heavenly hosts. Praise him, sun and moon; praise him, all you shining stars. Praise him, you highest heavens and you waters above the skies" (verses 1-4).

Many Bible verses reference the moon's beauty when praising God. Read King David's Psalm 8:3, 4: "When I consider your heavens, the work of your fingers, the moon and the stars, which you have set in place, what is mankind that you are mindful of them, human beings that you care for them?"

Solomon's Psalm 72 also sings God's praises: "May he endure as long as the sun, as long as the moon, through all generations." "In his days may the righteous flourish and prosperity abound till the moon is no more" (verses 5, 7).

Tonight let's invite God's hand to guide our paths as surely as He guides the moon.

Moon Days, Moonstones, and Moonflowers

People throughout history have been mesmerized by the moon. For example, did you know that *Monday* was named after the moon? Remember, though, God has created all these marvelous, purposeful natural wonders to point back to Him, the Creator who has brought it all into existence.

The Lord truly has created an infinite treasure of natural wonders to be discovered, all pointing to the fact that there is a Designer who is a lover of both purpose and beauty. Take, for example, moonstone, a precious gem that is named after the moon's milky, translucent appearance. As the face of the moon changes depending on the sun's light reflecting upon it, the surface of the moonstone varies according to the light shining on its smooth face.

When we look at the moon, so big and bright and far away, we might wonder what life on earth is all about. King Solomon asked questions like that and came to the conclusion that God is the only way to true happiness and contentment. "Remember your Creator in the days of your youth," he advises, "before the sun and the light and the moon and the stars grow dark" (Eccl. 12:1, 2).

King Solomon may have sat in his palace garden as he wrote Ecclesiastes. Perhaps you have your own flower garden and have seen a morning glory vine with its early-day blooms that close by the afternoon. If ever you are in a garden by moonlight, look for a moonflower vine. Its blossoms are milky white like the moon and only appear at night.

Our One and Only

Job offers us a poetic observance of the moon's beauty while also proclaiming God as the one and only God to worship: "If I have regarded the sun in its radiance or the moon moving in splendor, so that my heart was secretly enticed and my hand offered them a kiss of homage, then these also would be sins to be judged, for I would have been unfaithful to God on high" (Job 31:26-28). In fact, the worship of "created things rather than the Creator" is a well-documented problem in the Bible (Rom. 1:25). Let's observe the mysterious moon and give glory to the God who made it all.

Read John 1:17-19: "For the law was given through Moses; grace and truth came through Jesus Christ. No one has ever seen God, but the one and only Son, who is himself God and is in closest relationship with the Father, has made him known." What are your thoughts about the one true God?

What do God and Jesus mean to you?

Prayer Focus

Dear God, thank You for the light in the beautiful moon that reminds us of Your light. You offer us direction in the darkness and in the many phases of our lives. Today let us be a reflection of Your light to others. Thank You for all the wonders in nature, each moonbeam that streams down appears like a gift from You. We are grateful, and we praise only Your name, dear Lord. Amen.

Zoom Lens

Read 1 Samuel 20. What was the name of the feast David was supposed to attend? It gives us another sense of the ancient lunar calendar.

Action Shot

Read 1 Corinthians 15:40-42. To what does Paul compare the moon's glorious beauty or splendor?

The moon changes hour to hour, day to day, and month to month. Use a pair of binoculars or a telescope and, during the next month, spend some time gazing at the moon and spending silent time with God. When you gaze at moonlight, think of the true light in John 1:9, "the true light that gives light to everyone."

---

* Several English translations of the hymn exist. One version, for instance, instead says, "Thou silver moon with softer gleam."

Chapter 18

The Stars: Following the Light

I, Jesus, . . . am the Root and the Offspring of David, and the bright Morning Star.
—Revelation 22:16

A skyward glance on a clear night evokes wonders. Tiny pricks of light dot a blue-black sky. Some of us wish on a star. Some of us try to spot our favorite constellation. Some of us try to count them. Astronomers estimate that our galaxy, the Milky Way, hosts more than *1 billion* stars, but Psalm 147:4 says that God "determines the number of the stars and calls them each by name."

"God made two great lights—the greater light to govern the day and the lesser light to govern the night. He also made the stars" (Gen. 1:16).

Stars are commonly called celestial bodies and heavenly lights, but authors Ian Ridpath and Wil Tirion explain in *Stars and Planets* that a star is an orb of gas that is "born from massive clouds of gas and dust within our galaxy." The nearest star to the earth is our sun, which is 10,472°F (5,800°C), midrange in temperature between cooler stars, of 5,432°F (3,000°C), and the hottest stars, of 72,032°F (40,000°C).

Paul reminds us that each "star differs from star in splendor" (1 Cor. 15:41). And God told Job that when the earth was formed, "the morning stars sang together and all the angels shouted for joy" (Job 38:7).

Read Job 22:12. Who is higher than the loftiest stars? Who is in the heights of heaven? Let's gaze on other wondrous stories about the luminous stars of the night sky; they offer us a glimpse of our Creator's mystery.

Abram's Stars of True Faith

Long ago the Lord God made a covenant with Abram. He said to him: "Do not be afraid, Abram. I am your shield, your very great reward." But Abraham's immediate concern was that he and his wife were still childless (in those days having children was extremely important for many reasons). God answered Abram's concern in the following way: "He took him outside and said, 'Look up at the sky and count the stars—if indeed you can count them.' Then he said to him, 'So shall your offspring be.' Abram believed the Lord, and he credited it to him as righteousness" (Gen. 15:1, 5, 6).

Listen to another version of Genesis 15:6: "And Abram believed the Lord, and the Lord counted him as righteous because of his faith" (NLT). Abram shows us what true faith looks like. He "believed the Lord," even though it looked improbable that God's promise would come true. When Abram's wife, Sarai, heard that she would bear a child, she laughed at the absurdity of having a baby in her old age (Gen. 18:12). By the laws of nature, Abram and Sarai were too old to have children. But God was working to change Abram and Sarai's self-concepts. In Genesis 17 God changed their names. Abram became Abraham, which means "father of many" in Hebrew. Sarai, who saw herself as an old woman, became Sarah, a young "princess" in the Hebrew language.

Is there an area of your life you wish to change but can't see how? Have the faith of Abram. Ask God to help you see yourself and your situation in a new way. Then say to yourself, "I can do all things through Christ who strengthens me" (Phil. 4:13, NKJV).

Two New Testament authors repeat Abram's story in their definitions of true faith. Read James 2:23: "And the scripture was fulfilled that says, 'Abraham believed God, and it was credited to him as righteousness,' and he was called God's friend." Paul writes, "What does scripture say? 'Abraham believed God, and it was credited to him as righteousness'" (Rom. 4:3).

In expounding on their definitions of true faith, Paul tells us that we are saved by faith, not works. Read Galatians 2:16: "Know that a person is not justified by the works of the law, but by faith in Jesus Christ."

But James tells us: "What good is it, my brothers and sisters, if someone claims to have faith but has no deeds? Can such faith save them? Suppose a brother or a sister is without clothes and daily food. If one of you says to them, 'Go in peace; keep warm and well fed,' but does nothing about their physical needs, what good is it? In the same way, faith by itself, if it is not accompanied by action, is dead" (James 2:14-17).

Abraham shows us the way to put the cornerstone, the first building block, of faith into place: believe in the Lord. Paul reminds us that we are justified by faith in Jesus, but James leads us to put our faith in action. We must *live* as Jesus lived, by helping others. We are all "members of God's family. Together, we are his house, built on the foundation of the apostles and the prophets. And the cornerstone is Christ Jesus himself" (Eph. 2:19, 20, NLT). Read Nehemiah 9:23, in which the people remember the story of Abraham's descendants, "numerous as the stars."

11 Stars—Lighting the Way Toward Forgiveness

Genesis 37 tells the familiar story of Joseph and the coat of many colors his father, Jacob, gave him. Joseph had many prophetic dreams. In one of the dreams the sun, moon, and 11 stars bowed down to him. Jacob asked, "Will your mother and I and your brothers actually come and bow down to the ground before you?" (Gen. 37:10).

Joseph had a dream of God's great purpose for him, but everything in his life seemed to go the wrong direction. First, his brothers were jealous of the attention Jacob gave to him. And one terrible day Joseph's brothers sold him into slavery. He was taken to Egypt, a country very far from his home.

But "the Lord was with Joseph so that he prospered, and he lived in the house of his Egyptian master" (Gen. 39:2). When Joseph was wrongfully accused and put in prison, the Lord was with him again. Joseph soon found favor with the prison warden and interpreted dreams for two prisoners.

Two years later Joseph was called to the royal court to interpret the dreams that King Pharaoh had—which predicted an impending famine. Joseph explained the dream, telling Pharaoh that it was his (Joseph's) God who gave him the answer. Pharaoh was so impressed with Joseph that he put him in charge of stockpiling wheat to use during the famine. When the famine was at its worst, Joseph's brothers traveled to Egypt to buy grain. By then Joseph was the prime minister of Egypt, and when he revealed his true identity, his brothers were terrified. But at his urging, Jacob's entire family moved to Egypt.

After Jacob's death Joseph's brothers were afraid that he would reveal his anger toward them. But again Joseph showed his true colors, brilliant as the stars. He said to his brothers, "Am I in the place of God?" (Gen. 50:19). Joseph knew that only God has the power to judge. He also told them, "You intended to harm me, but God intended it for good" (verse 20).

Joseph's life is a humbling example of forgiveness, one of the building blocks for following Jesus. Joseph kept his faith in God, his eyes on his dream, and forgiveness in his heart. Joseph allowed God to fulfill the purpose He had for his life in God's way and in God's time.

Do you forgive people who hurt you? Can you think of times that you have been forgiven? Colossians 3:13 reminds us: "Bear with each other and forgive one another if any of you has a grievance against someone. Forgive as the Lord forgave you."

Following a Star

The Gospel of Matthew tells us that when Jesus was born, Magi (often called the Wise Men) saw a star in the east and traveled to Jerusalem to worship Him. Matthew 2:2 says that they asked everyone in town, "Where is the one who has been born king of the Jews? We saw his star when it rose and have come to worship him."

This angered King Herod, who secretly called them to his court to hear more about the star. Herod told the Magi to find the baby Jesus and report back to him on where he was.

Hear the rest of the Magi's story. "After [the Wise Men] had heard the king, they went on their way, and the star they had seen when it rose went ahead of them until it stopped over the place where the child was. When they saw the star, they were overjoyed. On coming to the house, they saw the child with his mother Mary, and they bowed down and worshipped him. Then they opened their treasures and presented him with gifts of gold, frankincense and myrrh" (Matt. 2:9-11).

Matthew doesn't name the number of Magi who followed the star to Jesus. We assume there are three because of the number of gifts they brought. Their gifts are highly symbolic. Gold symbolizes Jesus as royalty, a king. Frankincense, its resin often burned in honor of the Father, honors Jesus as God. Myrrh's scented gum was often used to prepare the dead for burial. Myrrh symbolizes Jesus' humanity and future death. The Wise Men in the story are likely priests, men of great knowledge. They may have been astrologers who read signs in the sky.

Modern scientists, historians, and astronomers search for a logical explanation for the sighting of the star of Bethlehem. In *The Christmas Star* John Mosley explains that astronomers look at the timing of Jesus' birth, historical recordings of astronomical events, and current knowledge of the universe's mysteries. Astronomers ask if the star of Bethlehem was a comet, an exploding star, a meteor, or some other phenomenon. Mosley's conclusion is "that the 'star' might have been an unusual set of planetary and stellar conjunctions culminating in a spectacular close approach of Jupiter and Venus."

The star of Bethlehem may also be explained as simply a miracle created by God. Imagine the heavens opening in a flash of brilliant light to herald Jesus' wondrous birth. Regardless, a glorious parallel exists between the illumination the Light of the world brings to our lives when we choose to follow Him and the Wise Men who followed the bright star to discover the baby King.

Prayer Focus

Dear God, thank You for the countless stars that illumine the night. In their mystery they seem to form a pathway to You. In their numbers they remind us of the unending nature of Your love. Stars help us remember that Your light can dispel any darkness in our lives. Remember us, dear Lord, and always help us to remember You. Amen.

Zoom Lens

Read Nehemiah 4:21: "We continued the work with half the men holding spears, from the first light of dawn till the stars came out."

Nehemiah was a king's cupbearer turned construction foreman. When Nehemiah heard that Jerusalem's great defending wall lay in ruin, he asked the Persian king, Artaxerxes, to let him rebuild it. Nehemiah and his men worked long hours and fended off enemies who opposed the rebuilding of Jerusalem's wall. Nehemiah 6:15 tells us that Nehemiah and the workers finished the wall in a swift 52 days!

Nehemiah saw a great need, stepped out of his comfort zone, prayed for God's help, and led the way toward accomplishing a great work in God's name. Nehemiah remembered God each time he prayed, but he asked God to remember someone else. Read Nehemiah 5:19 and 13:14, 22, 31 to find out who it was.

Action Shot

In Daniel 6 we saw God rescue Daniel from a den of hungry lions, but Daniel 7-12 contains Daniel's visions. Read Daniel 12:3: "Those who are wise will shine like the brightness of the heavens, and those who lead many to righteousness, like the stars for ever and ever." The hope Daniel offered then to the captive Jews in Babylon still shines like the stars for us today. Sit under the night sky this evening and stargaze. Pray like Nehemiah, "Remember me, God." Rest assured that God already remembers you. He knows your name as He knows the names of the numerous stars in the sky (Ps. 147:4).

Section Six

Time in the Bible: Two Seasons

There is a time for everything,
and a season for every activity under the heavens:
a time to be born and a time to die,
a time to plant and a time to uproot,
a time to kill and a time to heal,
a time to tear down and a time to build,
a time to weep and a time to laugh,
a time to mourn and a time to dance,
a time to scatter stones and a time to gather them,
a time to embrace and a time to refrain from embracing,
a time to search and a time to give up,
a time to keep and a time to throw away,
a time to tear and a time to mend,
a time to be silent and a time to speak,
a time to love and a time to hate,
a time for war and a time for peace.
—Ecclesiastes 3:1-8

Chapter 19

Summer: Gratitude in Action

As long as the earth endures, seedtime and harvest,
cold and heat, summer and winter,
day and night will never cease.
—Genesis 8:22

Two seasons marked the passing of each year in the Holy Land. Psalm 74:17 tells us that God "set all the boundaries of the earth" and "made both summer and winter." Psalm 104:19 reminds us, "He made the moon to mark the seasons." The days of sun are summer; the days of rain, winter.

Scientists today tell us that Planet Earth is tilted on its axis, and the times of "cold and heat" result from its relations to the sun. When our part of the earth is tilted away from the sun, our days are shorter and colder. When we're tilted toward the sun, our days have more heat and light.

Summer days in Palestine are hot and long, often passing with hardly a drop of rain, but the biblical time of heat is a time of doing, of being active, of accomplishment.

Read Mark 13:28. Which tree does Jesus say will show us summer is near?

The Biblical Year

On our modern calendar, June through October mark the parameters of the biblical summer; November to May, the winter. The early rains Scripture describes begin in November, awakening the countryside. Lush valleys turn green. Crocuses and daffodils prepare to bloom. The rains germinate the seeds that have dropped to the earth or been carried across the countryside by birds. Farmers are hard at work in their fields, planting vegetable gardens and seeds for the next grain harvest. Some berries and fruits ripen in December, and by January, anemones and irises begin to bloom.

February brings some trees into blossom, along with hyacinths. The warm winds of March encourage desert flowers to bloom, and irises and tulips color the countryside.

The late rains fall and then end about April. May brings poppies, thistles, and lilies into their prime while other plants are setting their seed. Many vegetables and fruits are harvested in June before the hot, dry months of July and August wither tender plants and turn them brown. Many plants take a rest during September, but a few set their seed at this time. From October to November the early rains begin again, starting the year's cycle over once more (A. A Swenson, *Plants of the Bible and How to Grow Them* [1995]).

Time of Harvest

Proverbs 30:25 tells us that summer is the time of harvest: "Ants are creatures of little strength, yet they store up their food in the summer." As summertime arrives, the wheat and barley seeds that farmers scattered last November are ready for harvest. Fruits such as grapes, figs, and pomegranates grow ripe for the picking. Women prepare fig cakes and other delicious dishes.

Many of the biblical proverbs remind us of the value of diligent hard work: "He who gathers crops in summer is a prudent son" (Prov. 10:5). Proverbs 6:6-8 says, "Go to the ant, you sluggard; consider its ways and be wise! It has no commander, no overseer or ruler, yet it stores its provisions in summer and gathers its food at harvest." And Proverbs 26:1 tells us, through a construct of negatives, or opposites, that rain does not fall in the summer. "Like snow in summer or rain in harvest, honor is not fitting for a fool."

The God Who Changes Seasons

Read Daniel 2. The Babylonian king Nebuchadnezzar's dreams aren't nearly as disturbing as the expectations he has of his astrologers. The king wants his astrologers to explain his dream *without* first knowing what the dream is! In other words, they are the ones who need to tell him what the dream is about and then interpret it for him. If they can't do it, the king will have them killed.

Daniel, a Jewish captive in Babylon, is next in line to interpret the dream, or die. So the first thing Daniel does is pray. He also asks his three friends to pray with him. When God reveals to Daniel the dream and its meaning, Daniel praises God. But Daniel doesn't leave it at a simple "Thank You." If you read Daniel 2:20-23, you will find him praising God for His "wisdom and power," for changing "times and seasons," for deposing kings and raising up others, for giving "wisdom to the wise and knowledge to the discerning," for revealing "deep and hidden things," for knowing "what lies in darkness," for the fact that "light dwells with him." He then praises and thanks God for having responded to his pleas about Nebuchadnezzar's dream.

What is your great need today?

Take it to God in prayer and praise God as Daniel did.

Summer's Threshing Floors

In the interpretation of King Nebuchadnezzar's dream, Daniel mentions a threshing floor in the summer: "Then the iron, the clay, the bronze, the silver and the gold were all broken to pieces and became like chaff on a threshing floor in the summer" (Dan. 2:35).

In Ruth 3:2 Naomi tells Ruth where to find Boaz. He will be winnowing barley on the threshing floor. A threshing floor, as mentioned in these two stories, is a flat circular surface where farmers thresh their grain. Sometimes a single family owned the threshing floor, but often an entire community shared the threshing floor, which made it a central location and meeting place in the village.

After farmers harvest the barley, wheat, or other grain, it is bundled into sheaves. When threshing time arrives, the bundles are untied and thrown on the threshing floor. Farmers lead donkeys or oxen pulling a sledge, or threshing board, across the grain on the threshing floor. This loosens the grain from the stalks. After threshing the grain, the farmer tosses the grain up in the air with a winnowing fork. Through winnowing, the chaff, or protective shells around the grain, blow away, and the heavy grains fall nearby. Then farmers gather the grain, clean it, and store it in earthenware jars.

Bringing in the Sheaves

Biblical harvesttime inspired the words of Psalm 126:5, 6, "Those who sow with tears will reap with songs of joy. Those who go out weeping, carrying seed to sow, will return with songs of joy, carrying sheaves with them." The psalm, in turn, inspired Knowles Shaw to write his 1874 hymn, "Bringing in the Sheaves," still sung in churches today. Hear the first stanza:

"Sowing in the morning, sowing seeds of kindness, sowing in the noontide and the dewy eve; waiting for the harvest, and the time of reaping, we shall come rejoicing, bringing in the sheaves."

Can you imagine a community of biblical men and women during a summertime harvest, working together under a shining summer sun, singing their own praises to God as they stack and bring in sheaves of grain?

David's Summer

David's heart is heavy at the beginning of Psalm 32, and he uses the image of summer's heat bearing down to describe the weight he feels pressing on him. Verse 4 says this: "For day and night your hand was heavy on me; my strength was sapped as in the heat of summer."

Then David describes the freedom he feels by putting his trust in God and leaning on God's power to make things right in his life. "The Lord's unfailing love surrounds the one who trusts in him. Rejoice in the Lord and be glad, you righteous; sing, all you who are upright in heart!" (Ps. 32:10, 11).

Prayer Focus

Dear God, thank You for summertime, harvesttime, and all the seasons of our lives. Help us to reap the lessons You have in store for us today. Help us to be gracious, grateful stewards of Your gifts. Thank You for providing for all of our needs, but thank You most of all for the bountiful gift of Your love. Amen.

Zoom Lens

Read 1 Chronicles 21:20-25. What does King David purchase from Araunah so that he can build an altar for God? How much did David pay?

Action Shot

Read Acts 14:17: "Yet he has not left himself without testimony: He has shown kindness by giving you rain from heaven and crops in their seasons; he provides you with plenty of food and fills your hearts with joy."

Luke's message is that God provides. He provides for our physical needs as well as our spiritual growth. Luke's Acts of the Apostles is the stepping-stone between the 12 disciples who followed Jesus and the church that follows Jesus.

How will you follow Jesus today? Find one way to provide for another person in Jesus' name. The provision can be as simple as saying a word of kindness or taking a friend for a walk one summer afternoon.

Chapter 20

Winter: A Warm Stable

See! The winter is past; the rains are over and gone.
—Song of Songs 2:11

In Bible times winter stretched from November to May, a blessed time of rest and renewal. Both the early and late rains Scripture speaks of occur during the biblical winter. "Then he will send the rains in their proper seasons—the early and late rains—so you can bring in your harvests of grain, new wine, and olive oil" (Deut. 11:14, NLT). Early rains fall around November, after summer ends, to help germinate seeds as the land gets greener. Late rains fall near April and are essential for the final spurt of growth needed for a healthy, productive crop.

The summer of 2012 brought a bad drought to much of the United States. When the earth is dry, and if the summer months have passed without rain, we long for the winter rains, the latter rains. Job used these rains as a metaphor to describe his life before all the tragedy he experienced: "They waited for me as for the rain; and they opened their mouth wide as for the latter rain" (Job 29:23, KJV).

Read Hosea 6:3. Whom did Hosea say we can count on as surely as the winter rains?

Let's end our journey through the Bible's nature stories by traveling to Bethlehem during a mild wintertime as the Christ child is born. This legend draws on the first miracle of Jesus' life, the story of his birth found in Luke 2.

The Legend of the Christmas Rose

Rose hid behind an olive tree in the green fields outside Bethlehem. Silently she watched her three brothers, shepherds guarding their father's flock of sheep. Rose was gentle and good with the animals. She would be a shepherd one day, but her brothers told her she was still too young.

The night was quiet and tranquil. Tiny stars dotted the ebony sky. Suddenly the heavens split open, and a star, larger and brighter than Rose had ever seen, blazed in the night sky. An angel hovered above the grass a few feet away from her brothers.

And the angel spoke. "Do not be afraid. I bring you good news that will cause great joy for all the people. Today in the town of David a Savior has been born to you; he is the Messiah, the Lord. This will be a sign to you: You will find a baby wrapped in cloths and lying in a manger." Suddenly a great company of the heavenly host appeared with the angel, praising God and saying, "Glory to God in the highest heaven, and on earth peace to those on whom his favor rests."

Rose watched her three tall brothers fall to their knees and pray. Then they whispered to each other hurriedly, and it was decided: They would travel to Bethlehem without delay with their most cherished lamb as a gift for the child. Rose flew after her brothers as if she were soaring on the angel's wings.

Across grain fields and dry dirt roads her brothers sped as Rose ran to keep them in sight. As the brothers neared the outskirts of Bethlehem, Rose's legs gave way. She sat in the grass beside a smooth, flat stone and cried. She was tired, hungry, and upset. Rose was determined to see her new King, the baby wrapped in swaddling clothes and lying in a manger, but she had no gift for Him.

Above and around her, Rose heard and felt the rushing, beating pulse of massive wings. She looked up and saw the angel for the second time. The angel smiled for an instant and just as quickly disappeared. Rose gazed at the ground. The grass near the smooth stone, wet with her tears, turned to snowy white blossoms. She scooped up the miraculous flowers in her hands and ran toward Bethlehem.

Her brothers had disappeared into the heart of the city, but Rose felt the angel guiding her to the stable. Baby Jesus, as His mother Mary had named Him, lay on a bed of soft hay in the manger. Her brothers' snow-white lamb lay sleeping beside Jesus, and her brothers stood beside Joseph. Mother Mary beckoned to Rose, and she walked softly to the manger. As Rose spread her Christmas roses around Baby Jesus, Mother Mary wrapped one arm around her sleeping Son, and the other arm around Rose.

After this, Rose's brothers picked her up and carried her toward home. She showed them the stone where the angel had turned her tears to blossoms. To her delight, one blossom remained. Rose picked the flower, cradled it close to her, and carried it carefully home. She planted the Christmas rose in her garden, and the clump grew larger and larger every day.

To this day evergreen Christmas roses still bloom in wintertime. A true miracle, the Christmas rose's blossoms sometimes freeze in winter's ice, but the shining sun thaws them crisp, clean, and new.

Prayer Focus

Dear God, thank You for the gift of Jesus' birth, and thank You for winter, a time to rest in the safe knowledge that we are Your children. Thank You for claiming us. Thank You for loving us. Thank You for all the experiences that have led us to this point in our lives. Thank You for this moment. Thank You for leading us toward our heavenly home. We praise Your name. Amen.

Zoom Lens

The Old Testament prophet Zechariah describes his vision of how the world will look when the Lord reigns on earth. Read Zechariah 14:8. During what seasons will God's living water flow? Winter is the time when things in nature rest and refuel. Deciduous trees lose their leaves and look dead; inside, however, the tree is still growing and even renewing itself.

Think of the "down times" in your life. Are you still "growing" during those times? How?

Action Shot

Snow, mysterious and feather-soft, is one of the most glorious parts of winter, and it sometimes falls on the Holy Land. To read about snow in Bible times, explore 2 Samuel 23:20; 1 Chronicles 11:22; and Jeremiah 18:14. Every snowflake is unique, like each of God's children. Treat each person you meet today with the wonder you feel when you see a snowflake, and say this silent prayer over each one: "I thank my God every time I remember you" (see Phil. 1:3).

Bibliography

Ackerman, Diane. *A Natural History of the Senses.* New York: Random House, 1990.

Baker, Rosalie. *In a Word: 750 Words and Their Fascinating Stories and Origins.* Peterborough, N.H.: Carus, 2003.

Bartlett, John. *Bartlett's Familiar Quotations.* Boston: Little, Brown, 2002.

Bown, Deni. *Encyclopedia of Herbs and Their Uses.* New York: Dorling Kindersley, 1995.

Brewer, Cobham E., and Ivor H. Evans. *Brewer's Dictionary of Phrase and Fable.* London: Cassell, 1989.

Bullinger, Ethelbert W. *Number in Scripture.* London: Eyre and Spottiswoode, 1894.

Cook, John. *The Book of Positive Quotations.* Minneapolis: Fairview Press, 1993.

Cooper, J. C. *An Illustrated Encyclopaedia of Traditional Symbols.* New York: Thames & Hudson, 1978.

Dickinson, Terence. *Nightwatch: A Practical Guide to Viewing the Universe.* Buffalo: Firefly Books, 1998.

Douglas, J. D., and Merrill C. Tenney. *Zondervan Illustrated Bible Dictionary.* Grand Rapids: Zondervan, 1987.

Ehrmann, Max. *The Desiderata of Happiness.* New York: Crown, 1948.

Evans, Howard Ensign. *Life on a Little Known Planet: A Biologist's View of Insects and Their World.* Guilford, Conn.: Lyons, 1993.

Flindt, Rainer. *Amazing Numbers in Biology.* Berlin: Springer-Verlag Berlin Heidelberg, 2006.

Fox, Emmet. *The Sermon on the Mount.* New York: HarperCollins, 1938.

Francis of Assisi. "All Creatures of Our God and King." *HymnSite.com.* Accessed Aug. 15, 2012. http://www.hymnsite.com/lyrics/umh062.sht.

———. "Canticle of the Creatures." *Apple Seeds.* Accessed Aug. 15, 2012. http://www.appleseeds.org/canticle.htm.

Geddes, Anne. *Baby Names Keepsake.* San Rafael, Calif.: Cedco, 1997.

Gleason, Norma, ed. *Proverbs From Around the World.* New York: Citadel, 1992.

Gough, Robert, and Cheryl Moore-Gough. *The Complete Guide to Saving Seeds.* North Adams, Mass.: Storey, 2011.
Grieve, Maud. *A Modern Herbal.* New York: Dover, 1971. 2 vols.
Heatherley, Joyce Landorf. *Balcony People.* Austin, Tex.: Balcony, 1984.
Henes, Donna. *The Moon Watcher's Companion.* New York: Marlowe, 2004.
Hepper, F. Nigel. *Baker Encyclopedia of Bible Plants.* Grand Rapids: Baker Book House, 1992.
———. *Bible World: Lands of the Bible.* Nashville: Thomas Nelson, 1995.
Hill, Steele. *The Sun.* New York: Abrams, 2006.
Hooks, William H. *The Legend of the Christmas Rose.* New York: HarperCollins, 1999.
Isbouts, Jean-Pierre. *The Biblical World: An Illustrated Atlas.* Washington, D.C.: National Geographic, 2007.
Keller, Helen. *The Story of My Life.* New York: Bantam Dell, 2005.
Kelly, Bob. *Worth Repeating: More Than 5,000 Classic and Contemporary Quotes.* Grand Rapids: Kregel, 2003.
Krupp, E. C. *Beyond the Blue Horizon: Myths and Legends of the Sun, Moon, Stars, and Planets.* New York: HarperCollins, 1991.
Krymow, Vincenzina, and M. Jean Frisk. *Healing Plants of the Bible: History, Lore, and Meditations.* Toronto: Novalis, 2002.
Lindbergh, Anne Morrow. *Gift From the Sea.* New York: Pantheon Books, 1955.
Lonik, Larry. *The Healthy Taste of Honey: Bee People's Recipes, Anecdotes, and Lore.* Chelsea, Mich.: RKT Publishing, 2001.
Loughmiller, Campbell, and Lynn Loughmiller. *Texas Wildflowers.* Austin, Tex.: University of Texas Press, 2002.
Lucado, Max. *The Lucado Inspirational Reader.* Nashville: Thomas Nelson, 2011.
Maggio, Rosalie, ed. *The Beacon Book of Quotations by Women.* Boston: Beacon, 1992.
Mosley, John. *The Christmas Star.* Los Angeles: Griffith Observatory, 1987.
Neighbors, Aileene. *Proverbs to Remember.* U.S.A.: Hallmark Cards, Inc., 1971.

O'Donohue, John. *Four Elements: Reflections on Nature.* New York: Harmony Books, 2010.

Osteen, Joel. *Daily Readings From Your Best Life Now: 90 Devotions for Living at Your Full Potential.* New York: FaithWords, 2005.

Paintner, Christine Valters. *Water, Wind, Earth, and Fire: The Christian Practice of Praying With the Elements.* Notre Dame, Ind.: Sorin Books, 2010.

Peale, Norman Vincent. *The Power of Positive Thinking.* New York: Ballantine Books, 1996.

Petersen, William J., and Ardythe Petersen. *The Complete Book of Hymns.* Carol Stream, Ill.: Tyndale House Publishers, Inc., 2006.

Pickover, Clifford A. *The Physics Book.* New York: Sterling, 2011.

Poilane, Lionel. "Symbolism of Bread." *Encyclopedia of Food and Culture.* New York: Charles Scribner's Sons, 2003.

Pope, Alexander. *Essay on Man and Other Poems.* New York: Dover Publications, Inc., 1994,

Ridpath, Ian, and Wil Tirion. *Stars and Planets.* Princeton, N.J.: Princeton University Press, 2007.

Roberts, Michael Symmons. *The Miracles of Jesus.* Grand Rapids: Baker Books, 2005.

Ronnberg, Ami. *The Book of Symbols: Reflections on Archetypal Images.* Cologne, Germany: Taschen, 2010.

Rose, Jeanne. *375 Essential Oils and Hydrosols.* Berkeley, Calif.: Frog, Ltd., 1999.

Rose Book of Charts, Maps, and Time Lines. Torrance, Calif.: Rose, 2005.

Sellar, Wanda, and Martin Watt. *Frankincense and Myrrh Through the Ages.* Essex, U.K.: C. W. Daniel, 1996.

Shewell-Cooper, W. E. *Plants, Flowers, and Herbs of the Bible.* New Canaan, Conn.: Keats, 1977.

Silvertown, Jonathan. *An Orchard Invisible: A Natural History of Seeds.* Chicago: University of Chicago Press, 2009.

Spence, Pam. *Sun Observer's Guide.* Buffalo: Firefly Books Ltd., 2004.

Steedman, Amy. "The Legend of the Christmas Rose." *Legends and Stories of Italy for Children.* New York: G. P. Putnam's Sons, 1909.

Stuckey, Maggie. *The Houseplant Encyclopedia.* New York: Doubleday Direct, Inc., 1999.

Swenson, Allan A. *Herbs of the Bible and How to Grow Them.* New York: Citadel, 2003.

———. *Plants of the Bible and How to Grow Them.* New York: Citadel, 1995.

Vamosh, Miriam Feinberg. *Food at the Time of the Bible: From Adam's Apple to the Last Supper.* Herzlia, Israel: Palphot, 2007.

Wachamann, Shelley. *The Sea of Galilee Boat.* College Station, Tex.: Texas A&M University Press, 2009.

Walker, Winifred. *All the Plants of the Bible.* Garden City, N.Y.: Doubleday, 1979.

Wells, Diana. *100 Birds and How They Got Their Names.* Chapel Hill, N.C.: Algonquin Books of Chapel Hill, 2002.

———. *100 Flowers and How They Got Their Names.* Chapel Hill, N.C.: Algonquin Books of Chapel Hill, 1997.

Williamson, Marianne. *Illuminated Prayers.* New York: Simon & Schuster, 1997.

Winner, Cherie. *Everything Bug: What Kids Really Want to Know About Insects and Spiders.* Minnetonka, Minn.: NorthWord Press, 2004.

Wollard, Kathy. *How Come? Planet Earth.* New York: Workman Publishing, 1999.

Worwood, Valerie Ann. *The Fragrant Heavens: The Spiritual Dimension of Fragrance and Aromatherapy.* Novato, Calif.: New World Library, 1999.